STEPS TOWARDS

EDUCATIONAL REFORM

STEPS TOWARDS
EDUCATIONAL REFORM

SOME PRACTICAL SUGGESTIONS FOR IMPROVING OUR NATIONAL SYSTEM

by

C. W. BAILEY, M.A.

Head Master, Holt Secondary School, Liverpool
Formerly Assistant in Method, University of Liverpool

Cambridge:
at the University Press
1913

CAMBRIDGE
UNIVERSITY PRESS

University Printing House, Cambridge CB2 8BS, United Kingdom

Cambridge University Press is part of the University of Cambridge.

It furthers the University's mission by disseminating knowledge in the pursuit of education, learning and research at the highest international levels of excellence.

www.cambridge.org
Information on this title: www.cambridge.org/9781316633212

© Cambridge University Press 1913

First published 1913
First paperback edition 2016

A catalogue record for this publication is available from the British Library

ISBN 978-1-316-63321-2 Paperback

PREFACE

WE are promised in the King's Speech (March 1913) a Bill for the development of a National System of Education. The Bill is eagerly expected, and much is hoped from it. The object of this little book of essays is to show that unless the Bill succeeds in making the most of the movement for reform springing from the schools themselves, it can but grant opportunities which will be incompletely utilised; and will fail to produce the Utopia some people conceive as likely to be created by it. What is required is to give a new energy, and a liberal support to the whole work of Education in all its grades; to inspire it with higher ideals; to lend encouragement to what is now good and suggestive in it; to inhibit and restrain what is now injudicious and ineffective.

There is a mistaken idea in the community that State organisation and subsidy can do this and all things else beside. The writer wishes to show how mistaken this view is. Further, that there is a distinct danger in increasing bureaucratic control; and that without more light and life in the schools themselves, further educational facilities will certainly mean more complicated organisation, but will not necessarily bring increased efficiency. There is always the danger of getting by legislation "the contortions of the Sibyl, without the inspiration."

It is strongly held by many well able to judge, that the general vigour of English Education has not increased with increased administrative activity. Some of the best features of a less highly organised state of affairs have disappeared. English Education requires at the present time something to increase its vitality and freshness. It is like a patient who is somewhat stale in tone, and requires change of air, nourishment and a tonic ; but may get instead of these merely more visits from the doctor. Its immediate needs are a health-giving faith from the general public, the nourishment of increased State aid and the tonic of a better knowledge of Educational Science ; let us hope that it will not get instead of these a further development of officialdom.

An experience bringing the writer into contact with schools of varying types and with teachers of all classes may, it is hoped, be considered some excuse for his rushing in with certain definite practical proposals where others display a more angelic reticence. He hopes that the Bill will give the craftsman a new sense of power, the idealist further scope for activity ; but he believes that in Reform from within is to be found the only effective guarantee that additional national expenditure will result in a better national system of Education.

C. W. B.

10 *May* 1913

CONTENTS

TO JOHN MacCUNN

CHAPTER I

The key-note to effective reform of education
in this country is development. Schools and
teachers must grow in power and usefulness.
Hindrances to growth must be removed. More
favourable conditions for growth must be established. Various parts of the national system must
be vitally connected, and progress in the whole
organic unity ensured. But the reform movement
must be from within. Unless the organism has the
inner power to take up improvement from without,
development cannot take place.

Attempts to impose reforms wholly from without, will be as unwelcome as they are likely to
be formal and uninspiring. A code has always
been a name unmusical in Britons' ears and

"harsh in sound" to teachers. We do not take kindly to whole systems of law, theology, or education. Our order is rooted in apparent disorder, and this makes for strength as well as for some appearance of weakness. It gives distinctness, power, and originality even to our mistakes, and dignifies our blunders as experiments. It has produced the state

> "Where freedom slowly broadens down
> From precedent to precedent,"

and has made us rather empirical in all practical matters.

Of all classes in the community, teachers are the most difficult to coerce, and not the easiest to convince. Teaching tends to isolate its practitioners from the outer world. They are less used to compromise and expediency than the merchant or the politician. Within their class-rooms their word is law. So it is sometimes rather bluntly stated that they are narrow-minded, and stiffnecked; that they are Ishmaels and unable to see matters fairly from the standpoint of national or local authority.

These things are partly true. But it would be truer to state that the teacher as a craftsman is apt to think lightly of mere theory divorced from practice, and does not readily tolerate suggestions from those who have not had the responsibility of actual school work. Also it is only right to say that he has been very considerably irritated by unsympathetic officials. He has in many cases been made to feel bitterly that he is the under-dog. His professional attitude is therefore some-what aggressive. But it is not true to say that he is fighting for the sake of mere obstinacy, or for his own personal gain. He fights too fiercely to be a mere partisan. He is in reality taking a stand for what he considers to be his professional free-dom, the right of the creative artist to do his work in his own way. It may be taken that when he attacks inspectors or other officials, he has always some real or fancied hindrance to the progress of his art as a predisposing cause to a state of war. He is in most cases perfectly willing to discuss plans and methods with other brother craftsmen. An argument with an inspector too often takes the form of a defence against attack real or implied, and an official suggestion appears not unseldom to have an element of reproof in it.

This difficulty exists, and it would be worse than foolish to pretend that it does not, as it is a funda-mental difficulty. Some wise *modus vivendi* has to be found between authority and individual responsibility. Where it has already been found, the way to reform is open and progress is now being made. The deadest places educationally are those where the hand of authority is heaviest, where schemes are most complete but enthusiasm is absent. "It is the letter that killeth, the spirit that maketh alive." In many instances progress has been made in spite of officials, instead of by their co-operation or suggestion.

This is because the right type of education official is difficult to get. He must be of broad culture and wide sympathy, with the gift of organisation, yet with such experience of actual teaching-technique and such an intimate knowledge of its problems that what he has to say is sincere and convincing. He must deal with statistics; but yet not be ruled by them. Uniformity is in the writer's opinion an admirable touchstone. The official who oftenest uses this word and most seriously advocates the idea it connotes may be set down as third-rate. Procrustes was the first to practise the maiming art of producing uniformity. A statesmanlike official will find his highest work in stimulating and developing individuality. The system he administers will be at once highly complex in its details, yet simple and inspiring in its aims. It was a bad day for Rome, thought Cassius, when there was in it "but one only man." It is a bad thing for a city or for a school when there is not such a wise administration that the work of government is distributed, and an ideal of co-operation is not being carried out.

Such education officials, then, as are required must be men of rare gift. They should be well paid. It is a hope of the teaching profession, at present but imperfectly realised, that these officials may be produced and trained from within; that they may graduate in the class-room before they legislate in the bureau. They will not be ready for such high office at a very early age, any more than judges or bishops are. And the teaching profession will never be as attractive as it might be, so long as the best offices in connection with it are held by those with least practical experience of its work. At present, the field-marshal's baton is not to be found in every common soldier's knapsack.

At the outset, too, the writer must protest at the unnecessary multiplication of junior officials, clerks and others, whose work is strictly speaking *unproductive* from an educational point of view. Much valuable teaching-time all over the country is at present being wasted by teachers who are preparing statistics, which again are to waste money represented by the time of the officials who digest and present them. There is far too much "red-tape" both in local and in Government administrative departments. There must be machinery, but it is only good in relation to the work for which it is called into being. Offices and clerks exist merely for the convenience of the schools where the real work of education is being done. Any money spent unnecessarily in the administrative departments is really taken from the executive departments where it is badly needed. An undue importance is attached in some places to forms, regulations, and instructions. It would sometimes be an advantage to compare the office arrangements of a local educational authority with those of a world-wide engineering firm. In the latter instance, every detail of office expenditure and energy is reduced to the point at which it can be proved to serve best the firm's main purpose, viz., that of engineering. Anything beyond this would merely impede the work, harass the actual constructors, and add to the work's cost.

Most of the difficulties between teachers and officials have come about by the establishment of the bureau. The bureau afterwards increases its staff, adds to its responsibility, and leaves the schools less and less power of personal initiative and judgment as clerks "accumulate" and teachers "decay."

Many authorities, on the grounds of controlling expenditure, control all the details connected with expenditure. They do not say, for example, that the school shall only spend so much on books or stationery, but they control, piece by piece, book by book, almost exercise book by exercise book, the school's requisitions. Fixed Requisition Lists of books and apparatus, to be used as a basis for contracts, in time tend to rob the teachers of all share in the choice of text books or other professional equipment. Interest in these matters is therefore deadened and an atrophy sets in. The net result is another gain to the bureau in power and influence, and another loss to educational zeal.

Attention is drawn at the beginning to this matter of administration, for unless there is established a proper co-operation between the teacher and the administrator, additional grants-in-aid by the Government will be used to increase the cost of the bureau. Could not the Government measure do something to safeguard the rights and professional powers of the Head Master? In any case, would not the Government attempt to decentralise control, to the extent of insisting that all governing bodies or sets of managers should have a real voice in the management of the school they are connected with? At present the power of many such bodies is illusionary, and Managers a title given to those with but little power of management.

Let us turn from the officials to the schools. Do our present arrangements make it possible to utilise to the full the reform influences on his fellows of the inspiring and suggestive teacher? Education is so much the result of influence and suggestion, that it is surely of the utmost importance to secure the maximum transmission of the best influences.

No one can honestly say that at present any serious steps are taken to secure this. Students of the various training colleges preparing for the Government certificate, or a University teaching diploma, have a privilege granted to them at a stage of their training when they are not fully qualified to use it, which is denied to their colleagues of more experience who are working in the schools. Special demonstration lessons are arranged at certain schools for the students' benefit; but very seldom are any pedagogic demonstrations available for other teachers. Occasionally in connection with some special subject, e.g. moral instruction or Bible teaching, a demonstration to a class forms part of the course. Only occasionally does an acknowledged authority on a particular subject in a University give any public lectures to teachers showing how modern views might modify the course of instruction usually given in the schools. With the great majority of teachers, their professional training really ends when their teaching work begins. Compare in this matter the young teacher with the young barrister. Once the latter is called to the Bar, his training consists, in part it is true, in getting up actual briefs and in making an increasingly successful use of his opportunities of actual pleading. But apart from these chances, often rare to begin with, his main professional work is to listen to his seniors. From them he learns, day by day, in their open practice in the courts. His forensic ideals are formed, his attitude towards his work made, by an inspiration from the leaders of his time, and he remains in the practising school all his life, even when as judge he presides there and regrets that the Bar is not so forceful and helpful as it used to be. Who benefits at present from the most brilliant lessons given in any of our class-rooms? The pupils of course: but there is not any general handing-on of successful procedure except through the training college facilities.

There ought to be more interpenetration of educational influence. Teachers ought to be allowed, nay *compelled*, to visit the schools of our continental neighbours, Germany, Sweden, Switzerland and France. There is an additional and special reason why this plan should be encouraged in the case of teachers of foreign languages. Indeed something in this direction is done. But it ought to be done more widely and on general principles of observation and enquiry, even more than for specific hints on language teaching. The Government might make grants in aid of this interchange of educational experience. Just now most of the more highly specialised and technical development of teachers is gained at their own expense, out of their own meagre salaries.

At present, interchange of experience is not common even within the limits of a single town, although an epidemic of measles has been known to send wandering bands of teachers to put in a little time at other establishments, during the closing of their own.

Of course, at the base of this suggestion for the creation of further opportunities for teachers of seeing high grade professional work, is the belief that such opportunities will be welcomed by the

keen people. There are many indications of a great
national interest in experiment and research,
especially if the latter is associated with adventure.
Experimental Psychology has given a new set of
data for teachers to consider.

But the fullest advantages of an alliance between the psychologist and the teacher have been
scarcely realised.   Yet it is probable that to
psychology teachers must go, in the future, for a
knowledge of what it is possible for education to
do for their pupils, and even, to a considerable
extent, for some indication of the means by which
it can best be done.

"How far may education utilise instinct?" "Is
there such a thing as 'general training'?"   "To
what extent is education affected by emotion?"
These are some of the problems common to both
teachers and psychologists, and in which both are
mutually interested.   Educative theory and procedure must in the future be, and has already in
some places been, profoundly influenced by such
work as that of Mosso on Fatigue, Binet on Suggestion, Ebbinghaus and Meumann on Memory,
and Thorndike on Formal Training.

To link up everyday educational procedure with
a rapidly advancing experimental science would be
a great gain, and the Government may do worse
than support Chairs of Experimental Psychology
in the Universities, making it obligatory for the
new professors to give lectures at times, at which

teachers engaged in actual school work may attend. At present, the influence of Experimental Psychology is filtering into the schools through the younger teachers who have just left the training colleges, and, as juniors, these teachers will not be able to do much to give effect to some of the more modern views they have received whilst training. It would be a tremendous uplift for education if a Sabbatical term were allowed to all teachers, on condition that part of it were given to professional enquiry, research, and training. The present writer can speak with enthusiasm on the value of even a short professional course of training, such as that of the Oxford University Vacation course, to a teacher whose experience and interests fit him to take the fullest possible advantage of it. This is a side of training that so far has been overlooked, and yet from which great results might be obtained.

Another agency for the improvement of the aims and plans of education, of which insufficient use is at present being made, is that of the official *conference*. There are many conferences of educational bodies, conferences in the main which emphasise the administrative side of education or ventilate matters of importance to particular sections of teachers. But the conference as a vital part of the machinery of educational efficiency has not yet been developed. It is the writer's opinion that more attention by inspectors of the Board of Education might very usefully be devoted to furthering conferences. Friendly conference might largely supersede formal inspection. There should be, of course, in every *school*, regular staff conferences where the School's aims and detailed plans should be fully discussed. In large schools, further faculty conferences are also necessary. But official conferences between teachers and inspectors in a certain area, to discuss general problems of school administration, or detailed plans for dealing with special subjects, would serve a very useful purpose. They would not be so official as inspection is, and teachers would feel under less restraint in stating at them their plans and views. Much of the more important of the functions of inspection would be indirectly performed by them. They would serve as clearing houses of local educational thought. Through the officials of the Board of Education, ideas would pass from one part of the country to another.

After all, inspection is really undertaken by the Government, *ad hoc* for the purpose of certifying the schools as efficient agents for carrying on a work, so largely supported by public money. In the Secondary schools, a feeling of greater freedom is experienced than obtains in the Elementary schools, because the "full inspection" of the Board takes place at intervals of three years or longer. The efficient school is then practically liberated to carry out its own work in its own way. Inspection by other bodies, such as local Universities, would very properly be resented by the schools. This problem will be referred to later on in connection with the relation of the Secondary schools to the Universities, and the proposed abolition of many of the present external examinations.

Inspection cannot create, but at its best only discover, and in rare instances inspire efficiency. At its worst it may produce an atmosphere of suspicion and mistrust, which will make real efficiency impossible.

Elementary schools have suffered much loss of independence and its accompanying resourcefulness by being over-inspected. Not only do the Board of Education inspect without notice, but the most important local education authorities have their own inspectors too. In some cases, organising teachers of special subjects have a special roving commission to harry the schools, fulfilling, it may be, similar functions to that of the pike in the German carp-pond.

The result is that at present there is a strong feeling amongst Elementary teachers that they are being driven. We are quite near to what almost amounts to a rebellion. The staff of inspectors of the Board of Education should be as small as is sufficient for purposes of securing a national efficiency. In Secondary education, at least, the work of the Board's inspectors has been done so well, and with such tact, that it has triumphed over a very strong natural prejudice against it, and the inspectorial staff has the confidence of the teachers and the local authorities. But the inspectors have been trained in Secondary schools themselves, and are in full sympathy with their aims and ideals. It is probably because, so far, the way has not been found by which to utilise, as inspectors of Elementary schools, men who have had sufficient working experience in these to command respect, that the teachers in the country are dissatisfied with the present arrangements for inspecting Elementary schools. Many of the present inspectors, coming to the work with traditions derived from schools of superior social standing, have not always treated the work of Elementary education with sufficient respect. The Elementary teachers are asking for less inspection, and for inspection of a different quality, inspection with an intimate practical authority and a greater sympathy. The Government could do much departmentally to help in this matter, and already there are indications of their intention to reform.

Government inspection could be usefully employed to-day in a scholastic territory hitherto unexplored.

At this juncture a great service would be done to the country, if the Government would decide that existing *private schools* should be inspected, and certified as efficient if they are found to be so. The inefficient private Secondary schools are a great national danger. But help and encouragement should be given to the efficient ones. These have played a very useful part in the educational economy, and will continue to do so. They help to create useful diversities of type and different lines of educational activity. Still one fears that "Do-the-boys Halls" are not even now unknown. Cramming establishments for Civil Service and other examinations require especial attention, at a time when so many of the pupils of the efficient Secondary schools are tempted to truncate their educational courses, in order to join them for short terms of specialised work. It would be interesting to know in what number, and at what ages, pupils of public Secondary schools are being captured now by these private adventurers, the Commercial Colleges, the "pirate buses" of the educational traffic. Something can of course be done through the new Teachers' Registration Council : but the whole question requires heroic handling.

This brief survey from a teacher's standpoint of possible reform, largely from within, and yet, as has been shown, with considerable help desired from without, would not be complete without a reference to three matters of outstanding importance, and depending mainly on financial considerations.

The first is increased financial aid for Higher Education, taking the form of the provision of Scholarships at the provincial Universities for Secondary pupils of outstanding ability. The second is such financial support of the Secondary schools as will enable the salaries of the assistant masters or mistresses to be commensurate with the important duties assigned to them. The third is such a diminution in the size of classes in the Elementary school as will enable sound educational work to be done there.

It will be useless building the educational pyramid unless the end crowns the work. It will be unwise to expect high and cheerful service from badly paid men and women. It will be equally foolish to expect intelligent methods to flourish when, instead of classes under instruction, there are masses.

How will these problems be dealt with? And in what order? But dealt with they must be if we are to have better schools.

CHAPTER II

THE CO-ORDINATION OF EDUCATIONAL AGENCIES

Present links between the Elementary School, Secondary
School and University. The hiatus between Elementary
and Secondary Education. National resources of capacity.
Present arrangements discussed. "Levelling up" advo-
cated. Advantages of smaller classes. Scholarships from
Elementary to Secondary Schools, and from Secondary
Schools to University. Increased national support of
Secondary Education necessary.

All friends of education in this country wish
to see "unity, peace and concord" between the
various grades of schools. Many desire to see in
each district a territorial arrangement of education,
with the local University as fostering mother, in the
midst of all the schools owning educational relationship to her. Some of the greater Secondary schools
will no doubt wish to preserve their traditional
allegiance to, and intimate connection with the
older Universities; but it is certain that the creation of provincial Universities has given a new and
hopeful interest in the problem of the co-ordination
of the schools in large urban areas.

These modern Universities have been, for some
time, in practical touch with the work of both
Elementary and Secondary schools through their

relations with both teachers and pupils. The Vice-Chancellor of Liverpool University has recently laid stress on the interesting fact that a large majority of the Liverpool University students begin their education in the city Elementary schools. Both Elementary and Secondary schools have been used as University practising-schools for teachers in training, and Head Masters of schools have been appointed by the Universities to give expert assistance in the work of training teachers.

Teachers in the Elementary schools, in increasing numbers, have received a University education in the various University Day Training Colleges ; and a recent development of much interest is the number of such teachers who have continued their University studies, even whilst engaged in teaching work, and have taken further post-graduate courses in preparation for M.A. and other higher degrees. There has, in these various ways, been created between the Elementary school and the provincial University a living connection likely to ennoble and dignify education from its basis upwards, and to make the education pyramid of sound structure throughout.

There has also been a friendly co-operation between the Secondary schools and the provincial Universities. University professors have served on Education Committees and governing bodies of Secondary schools in the University areas. Head-masters and mistresses of Secondary schools have been placed on the University Courts. The relations between the education authorities and the Universities have been cordial and intimate, and Secondary education in the large cities, at least, owes much of its recent development and growth to the provincial University movement. This connection between the Secondary schools and the local Universities is likely to be increasingly strong and mutually beneficial. There are thus bonds between University and both Elementary and Secondary education.

The real hiatus in the educational system has been caused by a lack of sympathy and co-operation between the Elementary and Secondary schools. Relations between these types of schools have been less than cordial. Some opportunity of a real knowledge of both types of schools from within makes the task of trying to show what arrangements should exist between them an interesting one to the writer, but does not rob it of its delicacy and difficulty. A proper appreciation of the value and claims of these groups of schools, the great caryatides of the state educational system, is urgently necessary, and calls for a frank and free exchange of well-informed opinion. One consideration gives encouragement. In this country, whilst we recognise acutely differences of opportunity both educational and social, we do, on the whole, agree singularly as to what, at its best, education stands for. Not the youngest Student Teacher would put attainment before character—at any rate in an answer to an examination question. Owing to the general diffusion of educational ideals, Arnold of Rugby has his influence on the village schoolmaster of to-day, and the Head Master of Eton is not unconcerned with the labours of the village schoolmistress, that "Egeria" whose dramatic teaching of history in Utopia Mr Holmes has made known to us.

But we have not yet, in this country, the full democratic spirit of America, where all classes of citizens send their children to the free public schools, in order to emphasise that equality of opportunity on which the American school system is founded, and which our school system so far lacks.

What we have to strive for until such an ideal obtains here is, at any rate, such a "catching of capacity" in the national interest, such a transference of the ablest pupils from the Elementary school to the Secondary school, and from the Secondary school to the University, that our great national resources of native capacity are not wasted by the unthrift hand of adverse circumstances. Modern educational science seems to show that it is very doubtful if we can, in our schools, materially increase the available sum-total of that high intellectual capacity we call genius. It is native and the gift of Providence. We cannot anticipate with certainty in what individuals or in what grades of society it will appear. This is a sufficient reason why all the genius we have should be recognised early, made to operate from as high a level of general attainment as possible, and thus developed to its fullest capacity in the nation's interest. We cannot afford to allow even one "mute inglorious Milton" to live unrecognised and die undeveloped. The tragedy of educational waste has gone on too long.

We can scarcely say, either, that the present arrangements by which free places and scholarships in Secondary schools are awarded from the Elementary schools are so complete and successful, that we have already secured a sieve whose meshes will serve to catch all the capacity worth caring about, and permit mediocrity to escape with a lesser opportunity. Many people have this quite simple yet erroneous view and build on it a further false doctrine, that the Elementary schools contain the less intelligent and the Secondary schools the more intelligent children of the country. If this were indeed true, it would represent a state of affairs which the most optimistic of us might well regard as hopeless, and would give some colour to a not unpopular "hewers of wood and drawers of water" theory, dooming the pupils of the Elementary schools to be the perpetual servants of their more fortunate Secondary brethren.

Matters are not quite so simple. Although many of the brightest of the Elementary school pupils over twelve years of age do get free places

or scholarships to the Secondary schools, yet there
are still remaining in the Elementary schools many
deserving and capable children, who are not even
entered for free place competitions, because their
parents feel that they are not able to afford to
spend the necessary amount on books and clothes,
which would enable their children to take full
advantage of the Secondary school course.   The
Liverpool Council of Education, which in so many
fields has done pioneer and suggestive work, is
now attempting a scheme of voluntary aid to
obviate some of the more pressing of these
domestic difficulties.

On the other hand, it is well known that in
the Secondary schools themselves, there is much
indifferent scholastic material, even in those schools
where an entrance examination qualifies for admission. Any parent who can afford to pay High School
fees may generally find some High School willing to
receive his child if the latter is not an absolute
dunce, although it is doubtful whether a state-aided
school ought to exhibit any such laxity in its admission requirements.

From both these circumstances, therefore, viz.
the detention in the Elementary schools of capable
children, and the admission to Secondary schools of
incapable children, it is probable that there will be
for some time a certain over-lapping, due largely
to social and economic causes; nor are we likely
to establish in this generation an "End-on" system,

clear cut in its character and automatic in its working, like that of America.

Our main business in the interest of reform, therefore, lies in attempts to lessen the differences between the two types of schools, frankly recognising that there will be an organic difference between schools dealing, in the main, with quite young children, and other schools whose work chiefly lies with adolescents. But this breach of the gap must be done, in the interest of national education, by a process of *levelling-up*. It is inconceivable that any real educationalist should wish to draw the types of schools further apart. In solving the problem of their co-ordination, a mutual understanding between schools of various types would be invaluable, and some kind of cross-fertilisation would have excellent results. There ought to be greater opportunities for teachers to pass from one kind of school to another. Experience in Elementary schoolwork ought to be no bar to Secondary School preferments, and Headships in Elementary schools ought to be freely open to teachers of Secondary school experience, where these are otherwise qualified for the posts. When both grades of teachers have received a University education to begin with, difficulties of transference will be greatly lessened. Much of the strength, hope and vitality of the educational system of Scotland is due to this freedom of transference from one grade of school to another, a real inter-penetration, a scholastic *osmosis*.

In the writer's judgment, the main difference, at present existing between Elementary schools and Secondary schools in England, is best described as a difference of *morale*, although, of course, there are obvious differences of attainment between the pupils of the different types of schools at the end of their respective courses, due to difference in leaving age and school curricula. But the most important difference is really one which on educational grounds is much to be regretted, and a difference which one hopes may in time be considerably lessened, a difference dynamic rather than static, and of manner rather than of matter, of point of view rather than of content of curriculum.

The Secondary school pupil after his course of training is, or should be, capable of independent and continuous work. He has learned something of the way to work for work's sake. He has the beginning of an intellectual interest, and has formed some social ideals. He has learned to play fair. He has taken some steps towards imposing on himself those sanctions of discipline which will lead him to a high sense of duty and cause him to sacrifice his own freedom for the greater liberty of his fellows. He has had many opportunities of developing initiative and self-reliance. Perhaps, as a Prefect, he has had some share in the government of his fellows. The generous social inheritances of his school and home environment have played an important part in this result, but it should not be forgotten that he has been taught in much smaller classes than the Elementary school pupil, and that he has remained at school long enough for the social instincts, which only develope in adolescence, to have had a full effect in developing in him a sense of *esprit de corps*.

The average pupil from the Elementary school is, as a rule, well-behaved whilst his conduct is under observation, obedient to the word of command, and in many instances keen even to cuteness in trying to escape detection of his wrong-doing. But it must be remembered that he has been a member of a class of some fifty or sixty pupils where artificial strictness of discipline, and an absence of opportunities for developing self-control are necessarily found. Discipline in the Elementary school under present conditions must be strict. Punishment is likely to be swiftly meted out. The good disciplinarian is one who, like the King in Tennyson's *Princess*,

> "With long arms and hands
> Reached out and picked offenders from the mass
> For judgment."

Punishment has often to be given in these circumstances as a warning to others, not merely in connection with its better function the reform of the offender. Trivial offences against class-room order are apt to be disproportionately punished.

There is no time for a very close examination into the underlying motives of school offences. But with smaller classes all this will be changed. There will be more elasticity of treatment possible. Instruction will gain in brightness and spontaneity as the pupils are permitted to take a greater share in it; and the emotional tone of class-room teaching will be pleasantly raised. It will also be found possible to give greater attention to the individual pupil. The School Record of each pupil will be more accurately and carefully kept; individual characteristics more fully observed and noted. This will be found a reform of great service, when at a later stage the pupil's career is to be determined. In fact, it is not too much to say that every kind of reform within the school, which makes for its increased efficiency, is encouraged and made more possible by reducing the school classes to a reasonable size.

Such a change for the better would also make it less necessary than at present for any development of the preparatory or preliminary departments of Secondary schools. These are really elementary in their scope, and a better Elementary school system would do away with the difficulties which have led to their establishment. Their extension would only increase unnecessarily the amount of overlapping between the two systems.

If some stress is thus laid on this question of the "levelling up" of the Elementary school advantages to a closer approximation to those of the Secondary school, it is because, if this reform were conceded, the whole educational system of the country would gain by it an increased energy. Better Elementary schools would mean more adaptable material for the Secondary school, more intelligent students for the University and better citizens for the community. It is not in any way implied by this that all reforms must be from the bottom upwards. The opposite process must also take place, and will be considered in its turn.

The question of transference by scholarships and free places from one plane of education to a higher is an important and practical one. Scholarships and free places gained in one district should be transferable to any other. It should be possible for each local authority to make arrangements by which *all pupils* in the Elementary schools who are twelve years of age, and have reached a reasonable standard of proficiency, should at this stage be further tested with a view to selecting the most capable of them for transference to the Secondary schools. At present the arrangements made fall far short of this. Some parents do not know that scholarships and free places are open to their children, and have not considered the opportunities such Secondary school education may confer. It is even to be feared that some teachers selfishly discourage their brighter pupils from competing for scholarships. In any case a reform in existing arrangements is certainly needed.

In this suggested "transference examination" there should be co-operation between the Heads of both Elementary and Secondary schools. A joint Board on which both were represented would be useful. The School Record of each pupil which, as has been previously suggested, ought to be kept with some care, should be available for the examiners. In doubtful cases a further *viva voce* examination should be held.

When it has thus been settled which of all the pupils eligible ought to be promoted, the question of the maintenance of these pupils should be faced. The amount ought to be, as a general principle, in proportion to the need. At present some at least of the money given to the maintenance of Scholarship pupils in Secondary schools is wasted in the case of pupils whose ages range between twelve and fourteen. In many cases no aid is needed at all. In other cases a more liberal maintenance is required at a later stage. It would be well if all the money available in any given area for Scholarships from the Elementary to the Secondary school could be pooled, and a general fund used as individual cases rendered it necessary. This would be really an adaptation of the Scottish system of bursaries of varying amounts.

It now remains to discuss that kind of reform which we may call reform from the top downwards. We have said that high native intelligence is a national gift and a national asset. It is of the utmost importance that the country should be served by men of character, talent, initiative and enterprise. In all departments of national service there is need for fertility of invention, adaptability to increasingly complex conditions, and scientific accuracy. The bounds of knowledge can be extended but by the few. Yet even a few first-rate men in science, commerce and manufacture might do work of an importance to this country which it would be difficult to exaggerate. It is to the Universities we must look for such men. And we must see to it that the Universities obtain a supply of material better than they are getting at present, and that the Universities themselves are so reformed, as to be enabled to give opportunities for developing this material to a much greater extent than is possible now. University research work and post-graduate education is of great national importance. These new University scholars must have been trained to a high level in their various Secondary schools, not only well taught, but so trained that they will be readily able to take full advantage of wider educational opportunities, and may grow to their full intellectual height. If these scholars are unable to go to the University without maintenance grants, these must be given to them as bursaries, and, as in the case of the Elementary school pupil sent to the Secondary school, these bursaries must be proportionate to private need.

Once it has been secured that all, or nearly all, the most promising pupils of the Elementary

schools have been transferred to the Secondary
school plane, national interest will then centre on
the possibility of taking such measures, as will
ensure that there shall be no leakage from the
Secondary school of this national capacity asset.
The Secondary school must yield up to the University its full tale of "lads o' pairts," and this for the
sake of the nation. It is not held that a University
education is necessary for all Secondary school
pupils. Not all are fit for it. The problem of
finding future employment for the average graduate
is not an easy one. It will be further complicated
should the number of such average graduates
largely increase, unless the general attitude of
employers towards education is more friendly.
But on the other hand it is of national importance
that the genius should get his chance. And there
need be no fear of his not getting work to do
afterwards. The Government would want a large
number of the really first-rate Arts men for its
executive service. It ought to recruit these from
the Universities in consultation with the University
authorities. The Civil Service Commissioners' examinations are quite as much in need of reform or
abolition as those of any other external examining
body which now interferes with the general
educational development of the country. The
first-rate men of other faculties, e.g. medicine,
law, engineering and science, are also sure of
responsible and remunerative jobs. It is "up to"
the Government, in co-operation with the local

authorities, to find the necessary money which shall ensure that all first-rate talent gets its chance.

This is probably the matter which has first claim on the nation's purse on account of its wide national importance. Half a dozen capable men might retain or develope in this country several great industries which would otherwise go elsewhere, and "follow the flag" of educational efficiency. How many schoolmasters and leaders of thought of to-day have told us, that what England has to fear from Germany is not so much the German fleet, or the German army, as the product of the German Secondary schools and the widespread and highly efficient German Universities!

A national grant for University scholarships is in the fore-front, therefore, of the writer's claims on behalf of reform. In Liverpool there is, at present, a spirit of keen interest and enquiry as to the right relations between the Secondary schools and the local University, and the problem of the provision of an adequate and efficient system of University scholarships is being seriously discussed, both by schoolmasters and by University men. These deliberations may, it is hoped, bear fruit in proposals of national importance.

But apart from this question of scholarships for the more brilliant pupils of the Secondary school, there are other matters of considerable importance to Secondary education which are awaiting the friendly aid of increased Government subsidy. Pupils are compelled by lack of means to leave

the Secondary schools far too early. The average
length of Secondary school life is too small to be
considered in any way effective. What would
encourage the Secondary schools most at this
stage would be a more whole-hearted support of
Secondary education on the part of employers.
If larger numbers of employers would take boys
of seventeen into their Banks, Insurance and
Shipping Offices, insisting on a high standard of
education, the average Secondary school leaving
age would be at once lengthened, and Secondary
school work strengthened proportionately.

There is, further, as has been already mentioned,
an urgent need for such financial aid to the Secondary school as will enable better salaries to be paid
to the members of the school staffs. At present the
salaries paid to assistant masters and mistresses
in Secondary schools are quite inadequate. A
teacher's emotional state is probably communicated
to his pupil with more certainty than the facts with
which he deals. Disappointed persons cannot give
enthusiasm to others, and badly-paid and discon-
tented teachers are therefore a poor investment.
We cannot expect highly-educated men and women
to undertake duties calling for cheerfulness, high
ideals and an almost pastoral care and sympathy,
if the salaries paid to them will not remove them
from a position of economic discomfort, and enable
them to live lives as decent citizens in the places
in which they work.

The case for the assistant master has recently

been put in a temperate manner by the Incorporated Society of Head Masters, and may be left in the words of an appeal the Society has just issued to the public, through the various educational authorities. "The low rates of payment that prevail in many Schools constitute, in our opinion, a very serious blemish upon our educational system. In a large number of cases, the salaries offered to assistant masters, who must be men of good education and address, are deplorably insufficient ; but although the insufficiency of initial salaries makes it increasingly difficult to induce young men of ability and spirit to enter the profession, the absence of a prospect of regular advance to a reasonable maximum is a worse evil. A young man may be content with little if he knows that as his experience and competence increase his position will improve, if he can look forward—as surely members of the teaching profession should generally be able to look forward—to marrying and bringing up children of his own, if he can count upon an assured future. But if nothing of this is possible to him, it is inevitable that the spirit will gradually die out of his work ; he will become not more efficient but less efficient as time goes on ; and no amount of material equipment in our schools can compensate for the depression of the teacher."

CHAPTER III

MORE WISELY PLANNED CURRICULA AND IMPROVED EQUIPMENT

General considerations. Curriculum of the Elementary School. Need for preparing children more "practically" for the work of life. Reforms in equipment necessary to secure this. The Secondary School Curriculum. Problem of equipment. The School Library a literary workshop. Employers and the Schools. A Liverpool enquiry. Specific training recommended to meet certain present defects.

A consideration of the relative importance of the various subjects of School instruction, and of the selection and grouping of these subjects to form curricula, has always had an attraction for Educational philosophers, reformers and administrators. It has even interested a Government Auditor, and added the "Cockerton" judgment to the list of standard law cases. But teachers have scarcely given to it the reflection it demands, probably because their work lies so close to the details of curriculum that they are not concerned with the theoretical considerations which ought to determine it. They are the users of curriculum rather than its makers.

Reformers, however, who nourish the delusion that school curriculum determines national efficiency and almost personal salvation, are always active in this matter, and there are still to be found a number of people who forget that "If to do were as easy as to know what were good to do, Chapels had been Churches, and poor men's cottages princes' palaces." Schools are always being told what they ought to *teach*, rather than what it is expected, by training, children can be made to *be*.

The "man in the street," too, has his views on this important subject of school curriculum, and writes to the newspapers to urge certain reforms. If he is dissatisfied with his clerks he pleads for a return of the "Three R's"; if the labour market is short he wants more manual instruction. His wife wonders where our servant girls are to come from. When too violent pleas are made for early vocational training, one suspects that there is at the back of them the desire to obtain cheap human machines for unattractive jobs. Such frank utilitarians have not even the faith in ideals of the village grocer, who hangs in his shop window the notice, "Wanted, an *intelligent* boy." Further, the parents of our scholars have their own views on the subject of curriculum, some of them from time to time asking that their children may be allowed to drop this or that subject of the school course of studies, or to take up other subjects more intensively.

Heads of schools have, therefore, constantly to

defend the structure of a well-balanced curriculum against alterations at the suggestion of faddists with a movement to serve, of employers with "an axe to grind," and of parents who wish to alter public plans for private purposes.

In the case of the Elementary School the Board of Education has laid down a list of subjects which are usually to be taken, and in an interesting prefatory memorandum to the code containing this list has pointed out that "the purpose of the Public Elementary school is to form and strengthen the character and to develope the intelligence of the children entrusted to it, and to make the best use of the school years available, in assisting both girls and boys, according to their different needs, to fit themselves, practically as well as intellectually, for the work of life." This standard curriculum may be varied to suit "the needs of the scholars, the circumstances of the School, or purposes of experiment."

The public Secondary schools, with no such official list of subjects given to them, are recognised by the Board of Education as efficient when they "offer to their pupils a progressive course of instruction (with the requisite organisation, curriculum, teaching staff and equipment) in the subjects necessary to a good general education upon lines suitable for pupils of an age-range at least as wide as 12 to 17."

We may assign varying values to the various

subjects of school curriculum according as we hold that: The child should be trained to take a helpful place in society; or, that the child should be trained to get his livelihood; or, that the child should be trained to develope his own personality. No one such view alone, however, is found to dominate actual practice. We know education is personal: we believe it will be useful: we hope it may be of social benefit. Whatever be the details of the curriculum we adopt, most of us feel that education is something profoundly influenced by high ideals of personal conduct and a generous love for the common weal, and that although our school wagon moves along the plane of everyday life and duties, unless it is "hitched to the star" of spiritual illumination and personal inspiration, it is a very poor thing.

The curriculum of the Elementary school, as settled by the Government, is a wise and liberal one, and might well be considered a safe instrument, in able hands, for producing the beginnings of "a good general education." None of the subjects it comprises can be omitted without loss from a Secondary school course, whatever be in practice the differences in handling these subjects in the different types of schools. It embraces English (including Reading, Spelling, and Composition), English Literature, History and Geography, Arithmetic and Elementary Mathematics, Nature Study, Singing and Drawing, Domestic subjects for girls

and in some cases Manual Training for boys,
Physical Exercises and Organised Games. Further
inspirational elements are supplied in it by the
permission it grants for Religious Teaching and by
its suggestive scheme of Moral Instruction. It is,
on the whole, cultural rather than utilitarian in the
stricter sense. It leads naturally to a Secondary
school curriculum although this is but its "subsidiary object." When once our national system
has been more perfectly adjusted, it is a question
for consideration and further experiment how far
it will be wise to retain this curriculum, in its
present form, for pupils beyond that age at which
they are drafted to the Secondary schools, and
after which the Elementary school therefore ceases
to be, in any sense, one preparatory for the work
of the Secondary school. It is not to be implied
by this suggestion that the Elementary programme
is to be cut down to subjects of mere utility but
rather that it might possibly be modified, developed
and enriched. For example, if the pupil is never
going to learn Latin, it might well be considered
whether it is not worth while, at a suitable stage
of his course, to teach him the principal Latin
and Greek roots used in his mother tongue ; or
Geography might gain in human interest by association with the History of Exploration; or, in the
upper part of the Elementary school course there
should be an extension of Practical Arithmetic and
Nature Study to include a simple acquaintance

with Experimental Science, as it is concerned with the phenomena and inventions of everyday life.

But it ought to be definitely known when he is 12, whether the pupil is to *finish* in the Elementary school or not. He should not be allowed to linger there until it is too late to make a fair beginning in a higher school system. At present one set of children leave the Elementary school at 12 on gaining scholarship transference to the Secondary schools: and at various times between 12 and 15 others wander into the Secondary schools much to the latter's inconvenience.

The Elementary school curriculum has already in the hands of enthusiastic, skilful, and resourceful teachers done an excellent national work. And it might be made more efficient still if it were handled somewhat differently. The same subjects could be made more effective from a point of view of training for life if it were possible to treat them more practically. The ideas and ideals it creates would be the clearer and more effective, if more preliminary work in the initial stages of its subjects were done through the concrete, and less through mere "talk and chalk." Instruction has been developed on lines suitable for keeping large numbers of children in the class-room "still," not for keeping smaller numbers of such children educationally active. Children have been prepared more "intellectually" than "practically" for the work of life. Why is this? We have previously shown that it is due in part to prevalence of large classes, and have shown how a reform in this matter would affect school instruction. But if more attention in future is to be given to practical work, it is, in the writer's judgment, necessary to make some changes in the Elementary school planning and equipment. A school workshop for boys, and a cookery room for girls, is an indispensable part of equipment for every public school, whether Elementary or Secondary, and it would be an advantage, in planning new Elementary schools, to provide rooms fitted with movable tables and chairs rather than with desks, so that Constructional Work, measuring work for Practical Arithmetic, Drawing and lessons in Observation and Experiment could be more conveniently carried on. More floor space and greater mobility and adaptability of furniture are required. This would enable the whole work to be more practical. Madame Montessori has shown us how much may be done for quite young children, by sense training under conditions allowing for freedom of movement. Whilst not wanting to see any unwise imitations of the Montessori methods in the Elementary schools of this country, yet one feels that our own school equipment is too rigid and our instruction too formal.

One does not ask for reform in this respect in order to increase the number of artisans or to train for trades too early, since the same sort of reform is asked for in connection with the Secondary schools: but indirectly such a change of emphasis in school work ought to lead to the creation of more and better workmen, less "blind alley" employment, and fewer youths only qualified to become second-rate clerks.

In the Secondary schools the problem of equipment is not so simple. We want more laboratory accommodation—laboratories for Practical Mathematics, Physics, Chemistry, Botany and Zoology, as well as Art rooms, Woodwork shops and Cookery rooms.

In the Secondary schools, the possibility of improvement on this constructional side of education, and its value in producing resourcefulness, adaptability, and a sense of achievement, have as yet been scarcely considered in this country; but the initial experiments which have been made by some schools are of great promise.

The practical work is found to support and help the intellectual work in all directions. For example, pupils construct a stage, design and make their own costumes and scenery, and then produce their own school plays on it. Or a large model of a Greek theatre makes an interesting job in the workshop, and is the source of clear impressions helpful in the right understanding of the *milieu* of Greek tragedy when it is used in the classroom afterwards. A fraternity of workers is established through larger pieces of work such as the construction of a bicycle shed or a full sized "glider," undertaken by groups of pupils working together. In fact, given a good workshop, many of the further problems of equipment and school enterprise are solved by its aid, and the school is rendered increasingly effective by its own efforts from within, if these can be made without disturbing the too sensitive imagination of a certain narrow type of trades-unionism.

If no differentiation is made in these pages between the claims and requirements of *girls* as distinct from boys, it is not because such differentiation is held to be undesirable but because one does not wish to complicate matters unnecessarily in discussing general considerations. The differences will probably be most acutely felt in connection with the problem of equipping the schools for practical work, in the light of the varying aims of the respective curricula.

The curriculum of the Secondary school is necessarily wider and deeper than that of the Elementary school, since it provides for a scheme of education for an age-range of from 12 years to 17 years and over.

The English of the preliminary course is enriched by more systematic study of the best literature of our own and other countries. One Modern Language at least is taught. The beginnings of an acquaintance with Classical literature are made through a study of Latin and, in some cases, Greek.

Arithmetic becomes more generalised; Algebra, Geometry and Trigonometry are taught. History, ancient, medieval and modern, gives a more general knowledge of the world's development. Geography has now a world-wide scope, a scientific basis, and an economic application. Instruction in Science branches out so as to include the various departments of both Physical and Natural Science. Manual Training for boys, and Practical Housecraft for girls, still retain their importance. More stress is laid on Organised Games and Athletics. There is a School Cadet Corps. The Arts of Expression find development in drawing, singing, acting, and dancing, and some attempt is made to develop good taste in Art and Music. Fuller corporate opportunities are afforded by the various school Societies and Clubs.

It is by a general plan of studies and activities such as these, or at any rate by a plan broadly similar to it in framework, that the Secondary school proposes to give "a good general education." The details of its syllabus may vary, and different "sides" of its work be developed in accordance with its own special aims and opportunities. A bias may be given to the whole course in order to enable the school to meet local educational requirements, agricultural, commercial or technical. But its main purpose is to supply a general education.

It has, however, like the Elementary school, a further object to serve, and its subsidiary

purpose is to supply a training course preparatory for University work for certain of the more
brilliant of its pupils. These pupils will require
to specialise in a group of subjects leading to a
particular faculty in the University. They must
not on account of this be prematurely deprived of
the many advantages of a wide general curriculum.

It is important that the country should more
completely realise that such a curriculum demands
generous equipment. The Secondary school needs
not only complete workshop and laboratory facilities
on its Science side; but also for its full *Arts* development, its library, its art room and collection of
great pictures, its auditorium and stage for dramatic
representations, and, if possible, an organ to lead
its music. All this implies liberal expenditure.

Further, the school buildings and class-rooms
of both Elementary and Secondary schools should
be worthy of the work of Education, pleasant to
live in, furnished in good taste, and such as to set
before our youth, ideals of beauty and appropriate-
ness. In an age where there is so much ugliness it
is all the more necessary that the school environment, should produce a sense of appreciation of the
beautiful.

Amongst the items of complete general equipment, stress should be laid at the present time on
the urgent need of securing for every Secondary
school a really first-rate *school library*. It is
difficult to make education committees believe that

the library is the literary workshop. They are willing to buy test tubes and balances, but draw the line at books of reference. Yet the school library's claim must be pressed. A library will cost a substantial sum to provide: but it will give opportunities for a cultural development of supreme importance. It will stimulate and aid independent work by the pupils in all branches of learning.

It should be strong on the English side, every branch of English literature being represented as fully as possible—legends, poetry, drama, fiction, essays and biography. Works of criticism should be selected from those that are in themselves literary. A good history of English literature, and a Classical dictionary should be included. The historical side of the library should provide standard works dealing with original sources and illustrative materials, biography, social history, the detailed study of particular periods, General and European history, historical geography, together with atlases, a dictionary of biography and other reference books. For Geography descriptive works and books of travel are most important. These are expensive and need to be added constantly. Works of standard French and German authors will find a place; and works in *French* and *German* on Geography, History, Science and Literature will be of especial helpfulness. There will be a special Science Side also provided for by Standard Works. If a full Classical education is not provided in the school curriculum, it is, all the same, necessary to provide for the presence in the library of the best Classical works in *English translation*, and this development of literature has lately had a great stimulus given to it by the Repertory Theatre movement. Works giving a background to the Classics may be used by History students also. Such a reference library, generously planned and constantly added to, will be found helpful alike to staff and pupils, giving freshness to the school's outlook on life and enriching its educational resources.

But we need to "educate our masters," in this case the employers of youth, and especially the employers of well-educated youth—our merchants, bankers, shipping companies, our local municipal authorities, even the Government itself, if we wish such an ideal as we indicated for Secondary schools to receive its due recognition from them. A demand for such a product must be increasingly made if a proper supply is to be regularly produced. There is always a tendency, mainly economic, for youths to leave the Secondary school as soon as a post can be secured, whether their school course has been satisfactorily completed or not. Yet, as has been strikingly said by an educationalist of standing, "the Secondary school is the only factory which is required to turn out articles ready for use at all stages of their manufacture." A high ideal, a generous curriculum, an effective course of training, are useless, unless we may convince the employers of its product to believe that the best is the cheapest.

Some prejudices against a higher education of youth result from the fact that many of the present employers have not themselves had its advantages. They belong to that exceptional class in the community which, by force of talent and sheer pluck,

> "grasps the skirts of happy chance
> And breasts the blows of circumstance."

And they scarcely realise what they themselves have lost by their want of better educational opportunities.

Other employers, on the other hand, who have had the high advantages of Public School or University education, have no knowledge of the impelling stress of narrow circumstances.

The rich boy of poor education has not been unknown in this country, but *the poor boy of rich education* is a new product; and the business world has not yet adjusted itself to him. He is, however, the Nation's hope and Lord Haldane is his fairy god-mother.

Some five years ago the writer, desiring to know what Liverpool employers wanted, or thought they wanted, made enquiry by questionnaire addressed to twelve representative Liverpool firms, comprising four steamship lines, two general merchants, one firm of brokers, a joint-stock bank, a firm of engineers and two solicitors.

These employers were asked what, in their opinion, were the school subjects of most importance to Secondary school pupils expecting to find

posts in Liverpool. They were asked to criticise
the present treatment of such subjects in the
schools. They were further invited to associate
more closely their views with a typical Secondary
school curriculum, by arranging the usual subjects
of it in a scale of values.

The firms were most kind and answered the
enquiries fully. Their attitude towards school
studies is shown by the following analysis of their
replies. Of the twelve firms eleven consider *legible
handwriting* the school subject of greatest importance to Liverpool youths. Arithmetic, especially
Arithmetic applied to commercial calculations,
comes next, nine firms giving it prominence, and the
Geography of the world is of high importance to
six of these firms concerned. English Composition
as employed in writing a concise letter is of much
value; and no fewer than five of the twelve recommend Shorthand. The majority of the correspondents only encourage a liberal curriculum by stating,
that although the aforesaid are the main subjects
specially useful in commerce, yet they expect in
addition that his school course should have given
the pupil *general intelligence* One employer at
least has a liberal idea of Geography:

"By Commercial Geography I mean a knowledge
of the trade of this country with other countries,
imports and exports, trade routes, the manufactures of different communities, and their necessities
and luxuries, coaling stations, emigration and im-
migration, *and all the reasons why.*"

One employer writing of Arithmetic, English Composition, Grammar and Writing says, "these may appear to you to be of a very elementary character, and altogether too unpretentious to occupy such an important position in my estimation, but I can assure you that no subjects can be put to more practical service in a commercial career. They are the very foundations upon which to superimpose a knowledge of all other branches of study."

The firms freely criticise existing arrangements. In the opinion of nine of them the handwriting of Liverpool youths is wretchedly bad, and the same severe judgment is applied to spelling, five authorities condemning this. One employer writes, "The handwriting and spelling even of the most intelligent youths fresh from school is in most cases simply appalling," and others write in a similar strain. It is stated that letters have often to be re-written, time is thus wasted, and clients are irritated. Even in Banking "cases are not rare where clerks have been debarred from promotion to higher positions simply and solely through their bad writing." Five firms adversely criticise the English Composition, Grammar and Punctuation, and attention is directed towards précis-writing, the drawing up of concise reports and ability to set out a clear statement. To write clearly and briefly, and to compose a letter of which the heads are given, are of first-rate importance in all business houses, and we are told that "comparatively few youths have this gift." Arithmetic, which goes with English and Geography to form the main core of the commercial education desired by the firms, appears to fare better. Three firms recommend more attention to the commercial forms in which arithmetical problems occur.

The relative order of importance of the subjects of a Secondary school curriculum according to these employers come out as follows: (1) Arithmetic, (2) English, (3) Geography, (4) French, (5) History, (6) Higher Mathematics, (7) Latin, (8) Drawing, (9) Spanish, (10) German, (11) Science, (12) Wood-work.

It should, however, be noted, in connection with this enquiry, that the correspondents did not state whether the youths they were at that time employing had been drawn exclusively from the Secondary schools. It is not likely that this was so. But the enquiry and the opinion it elicited are mentioned here, because they show the attitude towards school studies which, at any rate until a few years ago, the majority of English employers maintained.

It is interesting to contrast with this narrow utilitarian view the fuller faith in educational ideals shown by Mr Charles Booth of the Booth Steamship Line, who in Liverpool recently stated that his firm had determined to take no youth into their employment as a junior clerk, unless he had received a good general education, and was at least 17 years old.

The employers' testimony is valuable as showing the use to which school education has to be put in the world: but their ideas on the relative training-values of school subjects are from an educational point of view entirely unscientific. Handwriting, which is a special accomplishment, perhaps year by year of lessening importance as writing machines are more employed, is put first, and constructional work with all its opportunities for developing resource and achievement is put last. English supremacy in commerce will not be retained by mere handwriting. Yet since writing is the vehicle of communication in commerce, clear handwriting is as important as distinct speech. A bad writer stutters his way through commercial life.

The questions of Handwriting, Commercial Arithmetic, and Spelling ought certainly to be faced in the Elementary school and, if necessary, in the Secondary school also. Modern psychological investigations give a clue to the proper treatment. It is established that you must give a definite and sustained "drill" in any particular process of skill, if efficiency is to be secured. Mechanical repetition here counts for much. It is further proved to be unlikely that skill in any special task "spreads over," to any considerable extent, to another special task. If you wish a boy to do long tots correctly, he must practise long tots, if to write well, he must practise a certain definite handwriting style. But the handwriting will not help the tots nor the tots the handwriting, since special kinds of skill must be specifically acquired. This is where the coaching institutions have scored, and we must take a leaf out of their book. Any special trick may be learned through specific drill—typewriting, card shuffling, or even wagging of the ears, but such tricks are not necessarily parts of a good general education. If the school curriculum is founded upon even the most useful scholastic tricks or specialised tasks, its architecture is unsound. Your utilitarian, too, who requires the tricks will still demand general intelligence and "all the reasons why." It is not the business of the school to overlook the value of sustained drill of many kinds; but it *is* the school's business to prevent these from usurping the place of higher forms of educational influence.

Further, the youth, whose commercial value is at first judged by his proficiency in handwriting and arithmetical calculations will, one hopes, be required at a later stage to do work demanding a higher kind of intelligence; for, otherwise, what the employer really requires is a permanently second-rate human machine. What he will demand, if he is wise, is a potential junior partner—a youth of character and ability who will develope with increasing opportunities, and adapt himself to changing requirements. The employer who backs mediocrity is putting his money on the wrong horse.

CHAPTER IV

A SENSE OF VOCATION IN TEACHING

Teaching as an art. The Mind of a Child. The Teacher as Craftsman. Technique and training. The Science of Education. The History of Education. The "Teacher Element" in Poet and Prophet. The Ministry of teaching.

Effective Educational Reform must encourage and develope a deeper sense of vocation in teaching. The curriculum of a school determines the form its work shall take ; but the school's real success or failure is mainly determined by the teacher's attitude towards his calling. It is indeed difficult to over-estimate the value of the ministry of the inspiring teacher. His teaching is the sincere expression of himself, and carries with it conviction to others. He is profoundly interested in his work, and has the many gifts necessary to make others interested also.

The true craftsman in Education loves his art and is zealous for freedom to pursue it, so far as possible, untrammelled. He is, as we have shown earlier in these pages, restive under an authority which is unsympathetic, unacquainted with his practical difficulties, or that of the mere doctrinaire.

He is an educational artist, and resents being considered a scholastic artisan.

Like the painter, the sculptor and the architect, the teacher utilises physical things in the service of the intellectual, and the aesthetic and the spiritual; and like the poet to whom he is "a neighbour and near kin," he finds his highest material in "such things as dreams are made of." He deals, in his artistry, with that most wonderful and beautiful thing—the mind of a child.

The realm of a child's mind is one of fascinating interest to all its privileged explorers. It has within it "fairy fountains of the heart," and quiet gardens of reticence, breezy uplands of courage, and the swift running stream of imagination as yet untrammelled by experience. It has its "grassy places" of happy play, and its valleys of the shadow of foreboding sadness. And it has its sunlit heights where the soul of a child is alone with God.

From time to time, some inspired person has told us just a little more about it. To teachers of varying gift and work has the vision been vouchsafed —to the rake Rousseau as well as to the loving and blundering "father Pestalozzi," to the infant teacher Froebel, as well as to the Public School Master Arnold and to the psychologist Sully. Men of letters have flung open a little wider the "magic casements" giving a vista of it—Wordsworth and

Tennyson, Dickens and Robert Louis Stevenson, with many others, and in our own times Maeterlinck and Hauptmann, Kipling and Barrie.

A more systematic and formal survey of this realm has been made in recent years by a definite attempt at Child Study. Although some sensitive and child-loving people are, at present, a little shocked at the use of census returns and laboratory tests (the measuring poles and chains of this surveying work), it is obvious that the results of such a study, sympathetically and seriously undertaken, must be of the greatest value to the teacher.

There are so many things that we require to know about the growth and training of a child's mind. And if it is true that it is instinctive tendencies, and not acquired characteristics, that are by heredity handed on from one generation to another, and that therefore the business of education is mainly to lead up from impulse to ideal, an overwhelming importance attaches to a study of instinct. Instinct in this view is Education's driving force : yet our present knowledge of it is vague and incomplete.

The instincts of children need, therefore, to be carefully and accurately studied. It must be ascertained precisely when these instincts come to a height, and how they may best be "harnessed" for purposes of Education—how modified, controlled or suppressed. But without this knowledge, Education is dealing with forces it does not fully

comprehend. To the teacher, a knowledge of the
child-mind is as necessary as that of physiology
to the doctor, or of electricity and steam to the
engineer.

He ought further to be efficient in the technique
of his craft, for otherwise he will be a source of
reproach to himself and loss to others. If he has
not the necessary technical efficiency to discharge
his duties with success, he may hinder not help the
work of the school.

He must know his subject well. He will thus
be prepared for problems that arise unexpectedly
in the course of his work, and be able to satisfy that
reasonable enquiry it ought to stimulate and encourage. He must prepare and select his teaching
material, arrange it into convenient steps, and
bring it to an appropriate unity having its due
place in the general scheme of instruction. With
a definite aim set clearly before himself from the
beginning, he must arouse and maintain the attention of his class, and keep the members of it actively
employed. He should give opportunities to his
pupils to make their own contributions towards
the work, and should utilise the teaching devices
—questioning, description, illustration, narration,
experiment and repetition,—wisely and as required.
Each lesson he gives will thus be well worth giving,
will lead to something more complex and more
advanced, and will increase the knowledge and
power of the pupil. It is essential that he should

be able to control his class naturally, without obvious fuss or effort, and so maintain an orderly discipline.

In carrying out the above general plans, he will utilise special forms of teaching method. This is scarcely the place for the discussion of these in technical detail, but, in general, we may say that "method" is the teacher's means of carrying out his ideals, and becomes largely individual. General considerations will of course affect it, and science should profoundly modify it. But, in the end, each teacher's method will be essentially his own.

"There are nine and forty ways of constructing tribal lays,
    And every single one of them is right."

But it should be noted that Education has many aims, and may use many methods. Methods appropriate to one subject or one stage of instruction, are unsuitable for other subjects or for other stages of instruction. English school practice is fortunately eclectic, and any exclusive use of one method generally condemned.

From time to time a new method has given great stimulus and interest to teaching practice.

The writer believes that the heuristic method, which aims at placing the pupil for educational purposes in the position of an original discoverer, and which therefore utilises the curiosity instinct, is of real value in many departments of school work. It has been, rather foolishly, held to apply chiefly to experimental science, but surely the child may make important discoveries in literature, history and art, as readily as, or even more readily than, in science or mathematics. Exploring instincts should have a wide field given to them, since it is through them that knowledge is in the end advanced. To help the child to find out things for himself is to enter into a teaching partnership with him.

Yet to rely on heurism as the only effective method of Education, is to take for granted an unlimited amount of time at our disposal, and an insatiable curiosity on the part of our pupils. Further, children left absolutely to themselves in a science laboratory would discover nothing. Heurism always implies a careful dividing of problems into stages by the teacher, a suggestive limiting of methods of their solution, a real "shepherding" of the pupils which makes the so-called "discovery" in fact artificial. But even so such a joy does the gratification of this instinct afford that it cannot wisely be neglected. An important side to this work which may be called regressive discovery—such as in history would lead a pupil back from the policeman in the street to Magna Carta, or in science would lead from the dynamo back to Volta's experiment, has a useful place hitherto somewhat overlooked.

The "Montessori Method" has been held by some people to imply a revolution of existing practice, in its freeing of the child to educate himself without guidance or suggestion from the teacher ; and indeed the use by its founder of the term "auto-education" gives some colour to this view. But to wiser folk Madame Montessori's contribution to educational science, apart from her special devices for the sense training of very young children, has been to emphasise the principle, previously accepted by many, that the work of the teacher in directing, controlling and suggesting, needs to be further enlarged so as to include also a discreet *standing aside*, to observe, to give useful opportunities, and to encourage.

It is very doubtful too, whether the "direct method" of teaching languages is one capable of general scholastic application. It is obviously more suitable for young children than for older persons, since it makes more use of imitation than of logical analysis. A wise system of linguistic instruction would include both elements and many others. Further, our present knowledge of the value of "drill" in making automatic operations which are to be utilised in higher Education, leads us to believe that the direct method of teaching Latin and Greek will not be completely successful, unless there may also be provided in connection with its use suitable opportunities for mechanical drill in accidence. This would produce an economy in effort, although it may seem to some advocates of "soft pedagogics" a dull proceeding. Without it, the pupil's advance in higher departments of linguistic attainment may be marred by a slovenly and uncertain use of terminations.

The young teacher can learn much by observing the methods successfully employed by others. Even experienced teachers learn by this means, for the teacher who has no more to learn of his craft from others, or by self criticism, belongs not to the "quick" of his profession but to the "dead." Some help may, therefore, be given to him by a course of training. The prejudices against such a course mainly exist amongst old fashioned people who did not themselves have such an opportunity, and fail to see the necessity for others to get it. In some cases, their prejudices are increased by the extravagance of the claims set up by the advocates of training. But surely training may prevent teachers from making false starts, and save them much unnecessary experiment. Each individual teacher need not repeat in his class-room all the mistakes of his scholastic race. He may at least have the benefit of knowing where others have failed. Training moreover may have a high inspirational effect, and afford opportunities for observation of educational procedure in various types of schools which otherwise a teacher may never get. At its lowest, it is a preliminary canter over the educational course, giving a useful knowledge of its fences and ditches.

But whatever method, or combination of methods, a teacher adopts, it is not easy to say by what precise means a good command of technique is finally gained. It comes more readily to some than to others. In some instances, it never comes at all, for the teacher is both "born" and "made." The training of youth has always demanded from the teacher natural gift and versatility. Was not his Athenian prototype, the sophist, expected to be a whole specialist staff of teachers in himself?— "Grammarian, Orator, Mathematician, Athlete, Augur, Gymnast, Physician and Sage, he knew all things." The sense of artistic command of class-room resources, and of skill in the practical handling of his daily difficulties, is at once the crown of a teacher's work and his best reward.

In this country we are not, however, likely to adopt in its entirety and simplicity, the following contemporary American suggestion. "Mix with immortal youth and abounding health, a maximal degree of knowledge and a maximal degree of experience, add perfect tact, the spirit of true service, the most perfect patience, and the most steadfast persistence; place in the crucible of some good normal school; stir in twenty weeks of standard psychology, ten weeks of general method, and varying amounts of patent compounds known as 'special methods,' all warranted pure and without drugs or sizzling, turn loose on a cold world." Our conception is one laying more stress on the principle of growth, it has in it somewhat more of the *cutting, rolling* and *weeding* explanation of the excellence of the turf in the front quad of New College.

We would, however, make a strong plea that every teacher, whether "trained" or not, should make a study of the science of his calling. It is from this much true reform will emerge. He is bound to improve in mere facility by his daily practice. He will not by this, necessarily, grow in scientific effectiveness. Science ought to modify educational as well as other procedure; and the teacher who has no knowledge of teaching as an experimental-science, and for whom plan and device are settled once and for ever, is rather like a golfer who insists on playing with a "gutty" ball, because when he began to play it was the ball in common use. His golf may improve as he continues to practise; but he will find it difficult to persuade his fellow players who hear his strokes in the field, that he is not suffering from "old fogeyism."

In the writer's judgment, the association of methods of teaching with the experimental science of psychology has done something to make real evolutionary growth in educational procedure possible. Until quite recently, educational procedure in the class-room was mainly traditional, and was only modified by the courage of the more daring of the empirics engaged in it. From time to time, some one of these stumbled upon some improvement and handed this on to his successors. Education, like Medicine in the Middle Ages, relied

mainly upon a collected body of generally accepted
practices. It is more than this to-day, and has not
only established a set of doctrines generally held
to be a working hypothesis for future development,
but has further linked itself with a new Experimental Science dealing physically with operations
of the mind, and, by doing so, has pledged itself to
encourage, undertake, and profit by experiment.
Experiment is another touchstone, just as uniformity was held to be. The foolish despise it
and the wise utilise it, but in the end it affects us
all. Even the teacher who "does not believe in
experiment," may yet find himself using electric
light in his study, and travelling in his friend's
motor car. He will, of course, for the present,
avoid flying-machines.

We need more wisely directed experiment,
observation and enquiry more widely spread and
more carefully made, and a greater willingness to be
taught by the results of the work of others. This
will inevitably lead to changes in procedure. For
instance, if it can be definitely shown by experiment
that the retention of a passage to be learnt by heart,
is made easier and more permanent by taking the
whole passage together, rather than by breaking
it up into short passages separately memorised,
such a general truth ought immediately to modify
class-room practice, and teachers who refuse to
utilise such knowledge are fighting their educational
battles with bows and arrows.

Or again if it were proved that fatigue is physiologically a kind of nerve poison, which ought to be got rid of before it becomes too intense and produces a derangement of the nerve organism, just as one must constantly remove shavings from the joiner's plane, then the teacher who refuses to make an interval at the end of each teaching period is flying in the face of science. Or if the conditions of the successful formation of any habit as revealed by experimental investigation are :

1. Frequency of impression,
2. Strength of focussing of attention,
3. The absence of any " break " in practice,

may not all these laws influence our procedure ? The law of "non-break" ought certainly in character training to prevent many occasional weakenings, and even to modify the " only this once " attitude of the average parent. Schools where experiments in school practice are being deliberately carried out, such as the Fielden Demonstration School at Manchester, are doing valuable pioneer work for us all, and the creation of chairs of Experimental Psychology in the modern Universities would do more.

The History of Education is, in the writer's opinion, a subject more likely to attract and stimulate the experienced teacher who finds leisure for it, than it is to serve a useful purpose as a part of a preliminary course. We have seen that a knowledge of modern method is essential to him, but he is in his practice too far away from the work of the pioneers to appreciate their labours. At a later time, when he too has had his difficulties and overcome them, their courage and faith will impress him. The schools of history, the Academy of Plato, and the Giocosa (pleasant house) of Da Feltre, the Institute of Pestalozzi, and the Kindergarten of Froebel, will be compared by him with his own school and he will be able to understand their place in history; but there is a possibility that to the student in training the History of Education may merely be a chronological list of names of educators from Aristotle to Herbart, and a certain amount of information about these to be got up for examination purposes, even though he may cast a "longing lingering look behind" at what has been already achieved by others.

There will come a time when the problems the early educators attacked will appeal to him and indeed challenge his consideration, for these are the problems of all ages. For instance, Locke's dictum, "None of the things children are to learn should ever be made a burthen to them or imposed on them as a task," might prove a fruitful source of discussion to-day; and Rousseau's interesting plan of teaching experimental science to Emile might even influence the design and equipment of a modern laboratory. Rousseau's device will always bear quoting :

"I prefer that our instruments should be less

perfect and accurate, and that we should have
more exact ideas of what they ought to be, and
of the operations which ought to result from them.
For my first lesson in statics, instead of hunting
for balances, I put a stick crosswise on the back of
a chair and measure the length of the two parts of
the stick in equilibrium, and I add weights to both
sides, sometimes equal and sometimes unequal,
and drawing back or extending the stick as it may
be necessary, I finally discover that equilibrium
results from a reciprocal proportion between the
amount of the weights and the length of the levers.
Here is my little physicist already capable of
rectifying balances before having seen any. Among
so many admirable methods for abridging the study
of the sciences, it is very necessary that some one
give us a method for *learning them with effort*."

And this may be compared with Kant's view
in *Thoughts on Education* : "Generally speaking,
it would be better if *fewer instruments* were used
and proper children were allowed to learn more
things by themselves. They would then learn them
more thoroughly."

There ought, however, to be given to the
student at an early stage of his training, the
opportunity of studying those ideals, both ancient
and modern, which ought most to influence teaching
practice. No student can afford to be ignorant
of the Greek ideal of beauty and thoroughness,
of its sense of harmony, order and proportion and

of its high claims for citizenship. He should be able to appreciate the influences of the Renaissance on all forms of modern thought, and he ought to have a knowledge of foreign contemporary educational systems. But in the field of educational literature a discrimination should be made. Ruskin is, in the writer's judgment, more important to the young student than Herbert Spencer, and Arnold's Letters than, say, the Great Didactic of Comenius. He needs to form a standard of worth by the aid of which he may place his work in due perspective. He must know "the things that are more excellent" and press towards them.

Are the bishops and pastors of the Churches sufficiently alive to the importance of bringing all the spiritual influence possible on the students of the Universities, especially of those preparing for the ministry of teaching? No work should be considered more important than this. Voluntary agencies should be encouraged, special facilities and opportunities provided, and such work would bring a high reward.

The teacher craftsman will, in many departments of life, recognise a teacher-element. The poet will become a more richly endowed fellow artist. Thus Wordsworth's attitude towards teaching will make an appeal to him: "Every great poet is a teacher." "I wish to be considered as a teacher or nothing." The work of a teacher is, he reminds us, "to console the afflicted; to add sunshine to daylight by making the happy happier ; to teach the young and the gracious of every age, to see, to think and feel, and therefore to become more actively virtuous." Tennyson, too, will have a new interest when he is recognised as a suggestive and inspiring fellow teacher who knew how to make the lives of children beautiful and happy. "When he was a young man living at Somersby," writes his son Hallam, Lord Tennyson, in the *Memoirs*, "I have been told by those of the family younger than himself that Alfred was their delight. They would sit upon his knee or cling about his feet while he told them stories of his own invention that enthralled them, long stories of hair-breadth escapes, and of travels ranging over all parts of the world. For the boys he would make a Colossus of Rhodes, the fun being that they should have a 'thwack' from his open hand or escape if they could while rushing under the archway of his legs. Afterwards to his own children he was devoted. When we were still young he made us as much as possible his little companions. When the days were warm enough perhaps we sat together on a bank in one of our home fields, and he could read to us, or in cold weather he would play football with us boys in an old chalk pit, or build castles of flint on the top of the 'Beacon Cliff,' and we all then cannonaded from a distance, or he would teach us to shoot with bow and arrow. Some days we went flower hunting, and on our return home if the flower was unknown he would say 'Bring me my Baxter's *Flowering Plants*,' to look it out for us. If it were rainy or stormy, and we were kept indoors he often built cities for us with bricks, or played battledore and shuttlecock ; or sometimes he read Grimm's Fairy Stories, or repeated ballads to us." Such a statement is a veritable treatise on successful teaching.

He will find, too, a very real interest in the teachers of the Bible. Their consciousness of a message, and their faith in its ultimate success will inspire him to sincerity and singleness of aim. He will admire their forceful and sometimes rugged personality ; he will recognise the teaching devices they so freely utilised, their employment of the vivid, the dramatic and the concrete. He will see Isaiah walking through Jerusalem barefooted like a slave, and watch Ezekiel with his tiles portray a mimic siege of Jerusalem, or Jeremiah dash in pieces the earthen vessel. Parables will give him insight into illustration, and Bible narrative, "with its swiftness of movement, its sparing use of background, and its depth of feeling," teach him the art of simple and vivid narration.

The inspiring teacher with high ideals and a true sense of vocation is of inestimable value to the commonwealth. He cannot, however, hope to induce others to "follow the gleam," if he is himself "disobedient to the heavenly vision." In the words of Vice-Chancellor Sadler "the most essential things of all lie in the personality of the teacher—in sympathy, in moral insight, in an almost pastoral care, in a sense of justice, in candour of heart, in self-discipline, in consistency of conduct, in a reverent attitude of mind, and in a faith in things unseen."

The personality of the teacher is the main dynamic force in education, and on him is the main burden of reform. His work makes high demands upon him; but it has many compensations. It gives him the society of youth with all its hope, enthusiasm and happiness; and it keeps him young himself. To him is given, as to Great Heart in the Allegory, to "go before the children" of the Nation, and lead them into the "House called Beautiful." Surely, therefore, the Nation when it realises the value of the labours of such a "man-servant," will not treat him so meanly as to make the circumstances of his private life narrow and harassing because of his lack of a reasonable salary. This field of work has no attractions for the selfish or worldly, but it ought to offer at least the means of a comfortable livelihood—the labourer in it is "worthy of his hire."

But even apart from salaries, it is unfortunately true that the national estimate of the value of the teacher's work is not a high one. Teachers, as such, are practically excluded from civic or national honour. It is true a few schoolmasters have been elevated to the magisterial bench, as a reward for their political not their professional services, and a few high officials and the heads of Universities have received honour at the King's hands; but these exceptional cases do not amount to a Distinguished Service Order for the profession. It seems as if, in the great campaign against ignorance and vice, the only decorations at present awarded are those given to the Head-Quarters Staff and to the non-combatants.

CHAPTER V

A BETTER SCHEME OF EXAMINATIONS

Tests of school work necessary. Danger of mechanical tests. Present "welter" of Examinations in Secondary Schools. Consultative Committee's report on this subject. Criticism of the suggestion to establish a new Central Examinations Council. Reform should be evolutionary. Local Universities and Schools Examinations. Functions of the Board of Education in controlling and standardising School Examinations.

We have, as a nation, little imagination and less faith ; so tests abound. We have test tubes in our laboratories and test matches in our sports. It is true some tests are more easy to apply than others. It is easier to measure mere attainment, or dexterity, or mechanical craftsmanship, than it is to estimate capacity, or training, or artistry. A carpenter's work may be judged by something he has made in wood ; the product of the schools is a little more difficult to appraise.

But since the school aims at making its pupils proficient in various matters of scholastic accomplishment, and since it deals with the acquisition of definite information, on that side of its work, tests are useful and have always been demanded. Besides, even if tests are avoided during school life, they must be undergone afterwards. We must all be tested, sooner or later, in the world outside school. Some one will say, "You understand French? Read this letter then, and translate it from French into English"; or, "You are a musician? Play the accompaniment to this song"; or, "You have had a good general education? Prove it now by drafting this report, or criticising these statistics." The world is an impartial court of appeal sitting in judgment on the earlier decisions of the home, the school or the University, as of courts of inferior jurisdiction.

Still, it may be urged that a test of scholastic attainment is incomplete as a gauge of school efficiency, since it deals only with one side of school work, and further it is the more liable to error because it is a test of an intelligence that is immature and still developing. The older the pupil, and the more advanced his attainment becomes, the more definite may be the test applied, and in examination, a function of many variables, the less the possibilities of error through accidental or disturbing factors. It is, however, almost impossible to test a very young person's educational proficiency by such impersonal means as an examination, unless you reduce the test to a merely mechanical one. This is what happened in elementary education under the system of Payment by Results. All the children were tested every year at an examination conducted by external examiners, and their proficiency to read, write, spell and calculate, was definitely noted as passing or failing in a certain test.   A machinery for testing was set up by the Government, and the accuracy of its working on this low level was undisputed.   It did determine whether children could read and write, etc.   In a few cases, no doubt, members of the examining staff were tricked and the official brand obtained by fraud, but on the whole the machinery did the work set it with marvellous efficiency.   Its very success produced its overthrow. For, since the Government held that the value of the school to the nation was to be judged by the mechanical proficiency of the pupils, and this proficiency being the basis on which National grants-in-aid were paid, the schools became merely another part of the machinery—the producing side of it, and results were obtained with the certainty with which they were tested.   The whole scheme of national education was dismally mechanical ;   the schools became factories ;   intelligence was killed ;   ideals were neglected.   Even the zealous agents of the system are now ashamed of it.

There is the same danger to-day, in a less degree, in the field of Secondary education.   If it be generally held by the parents of the country, that the value of the education of the Secondary schools is to be judged by the pupils' power of passing Oxford and Cambridge Local and other external examinations, and there are indications that this is a fairly general view, then the Secondary schools, so far as they respond to this demand, will tend to become the other half of this rather more advanced but still mechanical and soulless arrangement. The schools will produce what is demanded. If the attainment of proficiency in a certain group of school subjects, as tested in a written examination, is to be regarded as the main work of the school, such proficiency will be, and is, in fact, at present produced. But this danger is just that which produced the *débâcle* in elementary education, a danger of taking the part for the whole and the "excrescences of the oak for its strength." The danger is, it is true, less in secondary education than it was in elementary, because there is not the driving force of grant-in-aid at the back of the external examinations system. It has been established by voluntary agencies, and may be kept in its proper place or modified in its aim and scope by the schools themselves. It has done a useful work and will continue to do so. It has only reached a dangerous position of undue eminence and importance through the possibilities it gives for unwise and misleading advertisement, and through a British attitude of mistrust of the un-checked. If our Secondary schools are true to themselves and to the ideals of the best and oldest of schools of Higher Education in this country, this external examination movement, which has only a comparatively short history, will never usurp the supreme influence in secondary education which examinations in connection with payment by results

did in the case of the other schools. Still, the
multiplication of external examinations, and the
gradual extension of their influence on curricula
and methods of instruction, have become so signifi-
cant that the Secondary profession and the Board
of Education have realised that the whole situation
needs to be discussed and the facts faced, if Secondary education is not to become completely entangled
in external examination, and school individuality
perish—the victim of its net and trident.

Public attention needs, therefore, to be called to
the Board of Education's issue of a Report by its
Consultative Committee on Examinations in Secondary Schools, which is of immediate and national
importance. The work of this committee has been
undertaken in admirable spirit and completed with
a thoroughness beyond praise, and is contained in
a volume of over 500 pages, to be obtained for
half-a-crown from His Majesty's Stationery Office.

The Committee's main conclusions have been
summarised in the educational press ; the striking
details may, however, "blush unseen," since the
number of subscribers to the Government publica-
tions is limited. The Report was issued in December 1911, and has now been fully considered
by the various professional bodies whose work
it concerns, and full justice done to its value, even
if some discovery of its defects has been made.
The general opinion of the teaching profession
is, that whilst it is admirable in its destructive

criticism, constructively it is unsound. It diagnoses the disease but fails to suggest a true remedy.

It is now proposed to consider this report in these two aspects and in some detail, on account of its tremendous importance at this juncture when reform is imminent and advice welcomed. In its first chapter is given an historical sketch of the origin and development of external examinations in Secondary schools in England. It is shown that this system is one of only 60 years' growth. Nomination and patronage did not finally break down until 1870, when the whole Civil Service was thrown open to free competition through examinations. These examinations have now developed so that in 1908 there were 37,000 candidates of whom 17,000 were from Secondary schools. University scholarships and fellowships at Oxford and Cambridge have, during the same time, had restrictions removed from them so that the field of competition has been more widely opened. And, further, the establishment of such bodies as the College of Preceptors (1846), Oxford Delegacy, and Cambridge Syndicate (1858) has given a great stimulus to the work of school examinations.

The Oxford and Cambridge Schools Examination Board in 1873 began their examinations for senior pupils of the Public Schools. The Universities, too, have had a share of such work. The London Matriculation examination, in its origin simply an examination for entrance to London

University, became used as a leaving examination
for many pupils who were not likely to proceed to
a University course, and from "this somewhat
casual use of a University examination as a school
examination," much has sprung. In especial in the
North, the Northern Universities Joint Board
Examination as a school examination has followed
its precedent. Other examining bodies are the
Society of Arts, the London Chamber of Commerce,
and bodies for testing special subjects, e.g. Trinity
College of Music, and the Royal Drawing Society.
Further, the various professions themselves insti-
tuted various preliminary examinations which
students shall pass before commencing their professional studies in Medicine, Law, Architecture,
Accountancy, etc. Special examinations also determine admission to the Army and Navy.

All these independent bodies, acting without
due co-ordination, have produced a welter of
examinations and in the second chapter of the
Report the Consultative Committee show the
salient points which emerge from a detailed study
of the way the present confusion works.

There are actually over a *hundred* different
examinations separately arranged for by examining
bodies, for which pupils of the Secondary schools
are entered ; and this variety is not due, or even
largely due, to variety of object. Most of them are
used as tests of the efficiency of the schools and
scholars. The examining bodies as a rule act

without any mutual consultation or any effective system of co-operation with the schools, or with each other, and amongst them probably the most independent examining body is that representing the Government, viz. the Civil Service Commissioners.

In quite recent times, i.e. since 1904, a certain amount of inter-changeability of certificates has been provided for. But, owing to varying standards and subjects of examination requirements, the present position is far from satisfactory. For example, there are only three instances in which one English University will accept the Matriculation of another, and the equivalence of examinations even when apparently recognised, is not effective in practice.

This is shown to have disastrous effects on the schools. Schools must prepare for these examinations or the pupils would leave them for *cramming* institutions. The specialising for these examinations prevents the schools doing their general education properly. The work is strangulated by this preparation for so many different examinations. Clever pupils are utilised unscrupulously to enhance the school's credit by examination successes.

This is fostered by the system of arranging pupils in class lists and honours lists, and giving distinctions in order of merit. In many cases not whole forms but picked pupils only are examined.

Parents are too ready to judge of the value of the school's instruction as a whole, by the special examination performances of a chosen few.

In the third chapter following on the foregoing conspectus, the difficulties and disadvantages of the existing system of external examinations are fully discussed. It is shown that examinations tend to restrict a wisely wide curriculum. Subjects not required for special examinations fail to receive adequate attention from pupils or teachers, although important from the point of view of true and complete education. Again, subjects flourish most in schools that lend themselves most readily to tests of a paper examination, so practical science, handicraft, housewifery, are squeezed out of the curriculum.

Methods of teaching practice are also restricted, as instruction must concern itself with the nature of the questions the pupil will have to answer, and this at the sacrifice of the teacher's individuality and that of his pupils.

Experiments in curricula and methods are discouraged. The making of any subject "focal" to the whole curriculum is prevented. There is a premature disintegration of the work of the upper part of the school. The various activities of a pupil's life outside the class-room are ignored. No use is made of the pupil's school-record. Mere examination success-hunting produces "an examination frame of mind." There is probably, in the case of girls, considerable nerve strain and loss of freshness and interest. The examination system does not keep pace with the developments in the best schools.

Further there is at present no official guide to the public, as to the merits of the schools as judged by examination, or any official machinery for equating and standardising examination results. Such is the sweeping and powerful condemnation of the present state of things by the Consultative Committee. And their verdict has been almost unanimously endorsed by the teaching profession.

In the last chapters an attempt is made to find a remedy, and certain suggestions are offered tentatively for consideration. No claim is made that by these a solution of all the difficulties has been made. Its main principle of construction is sound: it is that a better regulation of external examinations should be the basis of a necessary reform in Secondary schools. It is reform of examination and not abolition that is recommended.

Examinations are held to have certain good effects on the pupils, making them more precise and industrious, with the power of "getting up" subjects for special purposes, and affording by their results some standard by which they can compare their own attainments with those of others. Their bad effects are that they favour a passive type of mind, and divorce energy from creative process, originality or independent judgment.

On the teachers, well conducted examinations are said to have certain good effects too. They induce a thoroughness and completeness of instruction, they compel an attention to the backward pupils, and give standards by which the effectiveness of their work may be estimated impartially.

Their bad effects on the teachers are to limit the choice of treatment of subjects, to encourage the imparting of information in too digested a form, to give a wrong standpoint of success, and divert attention from the higher things of education which cannot be tested by examination.

"The cardinal point of any plan of effective reform" in examinations is held to be "the combination of the system of inspection with the system of external examinations." The rest of the Report consists of a plan for accomplishing this by the setting up of a new external examining and inspecting body, a widely representative examinations *council* to do away with all others. Such a council should include representatives of the Universities, of the Local Authorities, the Board of Education's officers and of the teachers, together with a "limited number of persons of practical experience, especially of the requirements of professional, industrial life." "The functions of the Council would be the supervision of all external examinations in recognised Secondary schools. It would lay down regulations as to the scope, time and methods of these examinations. It would

control their organisation, fix the fees to be charged
for admission to them, and approve the examiners.
The headquarters of the Council would be in
London and within convenient reach of the Board
of Education."

This bureau would of course act through other
and smaller bureaux. In each district would be
set up a local office of the Secondary school
Inspectorate with a clerical staff. In each of these
offices there "would gradually accumulate a mass
of useful information."

"Interview examiners" for the bureau would
visit the schools, inspect them, criticise their
methods, review their work, examine their candidates yearly, and issue certificates of proficiency
having the official *imprimatur* of the Board of
Education. Two certificates would be issued : a
school certificate for pupils of at least 16 who have
attended a Secondary school for 3 years, and a
lower certificate or testamur for successful pupils
who are not able to remain at school long enough
to obtain the full certificate. Further provision is
suggested for a higher certificate suitable for pupils
of 18. Suggestions for the conduct of such a
projected scheme of examinations are given in
detail.

Now the first great objection to such a scheme
is that it is revolutionary and not evolutionary.
It attempts too much. It abolishes existing examination tests and substitutes a new and untried

one. It condemns the present large examination boards, and then manufactures a new one more composite and unwieldy than any now existing. In a single paragraph it does away with institutions whose services to education have been for many years of great value. They are supposed to vanish as readily as did clan-Alpine's warriors when Roderick Dhu waved his hand.

Beginning with a safe general principle that there should be a reform in external examinations, it tacks on to this the controversial and, to many teachers, irritating contention that, in any new scheme of external examinations, there must be an association of inspection with examination. It only realises the value of the services of the inspiring teacher so far as these may be discovered and appreciated by the inspector. What it wishes to gain is an examination having elasticity, and a standard value, an examination intimately associated with the school work and in accordance with its general bias. It can see only one solution for this, viz. the linking of inspection with examination. It fails to see the better way of connecting *teaching itself* with examination. It does not approach reform by the wise steps of utilisation of existing forces, and reconciliation of conflicting interests. It ignores the possibility of educational growth and development untrammelled by officialdom. It aims at devising means whereby "greater freedom is secured to the schools." Yet it creates a bureau!

The teaching profession therefore will have none of it. At the annual meeting of the Incorporate Association of Head Masters in December 1912, the following resolutions were unanimously passed: that

(1) This Association welcomes the Report of the Consultative Committee on Examinations in Secondary schools as a complete and incontrovertible presentment of the injury done to Secondary Education by the present multiplicity of external examinations.

(2) The Association *cannot, however, approve of the establishment of a new composite Examination Council,* being of the opinion that the responsibility for determining the number and character of external examinations in Secondary schools should lie with the Board of Education.

(3) The Association requests the Board of Education, in co-operation with the Teacher's Registration Council, to confer with the Universities and Professional Bodies with a view to the institution of common entrance examinations.

Further resolutions dealt with the proposed new certificates, welcoming a Secondary school Certificate if accepted by Universities and Professional Bodies, but objecting to the "absolutely unworkable" methods proposed by the Consultative Committee for awarding it and emphasising the need to associate teaching with examination.

Some more practical plan is, therefore, necessary, and it is to the Board of Education that teachers are now looking to deal judiciously with the whole problem.

It is further important to discover how far the expert services of the teacher and the School Record of the pupil's ability and progress may both be utilised, in making external examinations more elastic, personal and convincing.

Let us take first the case of a large Secondary school with a strong specialist staff and situated within the area of a modern University. How may it, for example, secure a school certificate examination of Matriculation standard qualifying for admission to the professions, adapted to its own curriculum, and utilising its own record of its pupil's work? The answer to this, suggested by the present plans of London University and the Northern Universities, is that such an examination is, in a great measure, already possible. Boards on which Secondary schools are represented have been formed, which would provide the machinery necessary for the initiation of such examinations. The present arrangements are not finally satisfactory but they are suggestive. The Northern Universities scheme gives teachers equal representation on these Joint Boards with the University staff. In Liverpool there is a strong feeling that the development of such a scheme, especially with due provision for the utilising of the pupil's School

Record, with the employment of the school specialists as internal examiners and of the University staff as external examiners in close co-operation and consultation with the school authorities, but without any right of formal inspection or control of school method, should prove the key to a great difficulty. This would be, it is thought by many, an ideal arrangement for testing the work of the pupils of such a school at the age of 16 or 17, and at the end of a general school course of at least four years' duration. It should be the business of the Board of Education to promote such arrangements, to standardise them, and equate them with similar arrangements in other University centres throughout the country. Such examina-tions would plainly indicate how many of the school's pupils had received a "good general education," and might further show which of these was really capable of entering on a work of a more highly specialised nature, to be undertaken in the Sixth Form of the school in preparation for a University course which should be begun not earlier than at 18 years.

Such selected pupils should be retained at the schools without further fee and with help towards maintenance where such arrangements are financially necessary; for it is to such people that the Universities will look later for their pupils of distinction. They ought to be the University Scholars.

By such suggested co-operation with the teaching staff of the school, and by the right use of the pupils' School Records it would not be difficult to catch high capacity at a stage when a general course is complete, and it would stimulate the schools, the writer believes, to come into closer contact with the Universities, as it would help the Universities to be in closer association with the selection of the material with which they have to work.

Such an arrangement would closely resemble the plan outlined for a transference from the Elementary school to the Secondary school of pupils at about 12 years, who are discovered to be worth a higher education at the State's charge. It would be a second stage of the great national *sievings* for capacity and the more effective it was, the better would the University education become.

Further, its utilising of the principal assistants in the school, acting for this examination as accredited examiners of the University, would increase the *morale* and interest of the teaching staff. The men selected for such work would rise to their opportunities, and their authority and influence in the school would be increased. It is inconceivable that such a trust would be abused. A proper emphasis would also be placed on the pupil's record of work from day to day, the rewards of cramming would be diminished, tests of proficiency made more secure.

For such well placed schools with specialist staffs, such an association with the local University would prove mutually beneficial and stimulating to a high degree. Such a scheme utilises existing resources, promotes local educational unity, adds to the dignity of the teaching profession, and avoids unnecessary increase of outside control.

But there are other schools to whom such a scheme is frankly impossible. The small country Grammar school with its staff of three or four general practitioners, its remoteness from the Urban Universities, its own difficulties of curriculum, is obviously not now able to take advantage of such a scheme. Here the Board of Education must come in and decide which of the existing external examinations such a school may wisely utilise. Such a school is not likely to be engaged to any extent in heroic experiment, or in attempting schemes of work for which no provision at all is made by the present existing hundred examinations.

There will be schools, too, where the staff are unwilling to undertake the responsibility of acting as internal examiners, and Heads of schools who prefer purely external tests of their work. It is not suggested either that even with the most perfect machinery for conducting examinations, by examination you can ever test *all* that the school does or aims at doing for its pupils. A test of proficiency in certain subjects of instruction may, however, be a useful one so far as it goes. It ought not to be used as implying for school or pupil more than what it actually means. Since many schools will for some time require to use the Locals, it would be a beginning of reform if the authorities of the Oxford and Cambridge Locals were to yield to the pressure of high scholastic opinion, and abolish those class lists in order of merit which enable their certificates to be used for purposes of unjustifiable advertisement. Such a step would at once have good effect. In our educational system, as in gardening, exhibiting at shows is dangerous. Instead of the gardener studying the garden's general possibilities and arrangement, his only interest is in winning prizes and in forcing plants for show purposes.

The Board of Education, too, ought to set about the work of converting the professional bodies, and perhaps incidentally, of converting their own colleagues of the Civil Service Commission also. Why should not the Universities be more used to supply the Nation's more highly educated officials? When every clever boy in the country has had a chance of a University education, there will then be no need for the Civil Service Commissioners to act on the assumption that there are large numbers of youths to be selected for the nation's service without the Universities' aid. The lower grades of the Civil Service might also be recruited from the schools, and the School's Leaving Certificate be given a direct value in connection with applications for such posts. We are asking other employers and the professions to rely on such a certificate, why should not the Government itself give it some recognition?

The question of examinations is of importance in all grades of education. It should not be overlooked in the Elementary schools. Some means should be devised for testing the efficiency of the instruction in these schools, without turning the whole school system into a results-grinding machine. Here again the internal examinations by the school staff should have full weight, and in every case a careful record should be kept of the progress and attainment of each pupil.

Examinations have, in especial, the useful function that they draw attention to the pupil as an individual. It is not possible to organise public instruction for the separate and distinct benefit of each individual; but the system which secures most attention to the individual, which recognises, encourages and records his talent, bent and attainment, is the system to aim at.

Education has been cynically termed "neither a science, nor an art, but a dodge—that of finding suitable work for the pupil to do." It needs to be supplemented by the further dodge—that of seeing that the pupil does the work found for him.

CHAPTER VI

AN EXTENSION OF THE INFLUENCE OF THE SCHOOLS

Social and personal aims of education. Present weakness of Elementary education. Continuation schools and recreation. The ward club. Secondary school influence. Need for fuller co-operation and better understanding between the classes. Ideals of National unity. Influence of Literature and Religion.

The greatest educational reform from within would be an extension of the School's influence both by widening and deepening it. School life is at present all too short and the influence of school is not deep enough. In many instances the Elementary pupil leaves school at 13, and the Secondary pupil before 16, so the fateful years of adolescence are comparatively unguarded.

If Education is in great part concerned with human relationships, its possibilities for training in these relationships need to be extended and enriched. It ought to strengthen and direct, not merely such relationships as those of obedience and authority between pupil and teacher, but those of mutual consideration and friendship between these and that of *camaraderie* between pupil and pupil; to develope a better understanding between the various classes of the community, and an honourable intercourse between the sexes; it should foster the duties of citizenship and train for the responsibilities of Empire.

The pupil must therefore remain in the school fellowship long enough to learn its corporate lessons, so that when his circle of relationships is widened he may more readily take his proper part in the fuller life of college and of University, of profession, or of craft, of city and of country.

This social education will take two main directions, one, that of self-repression and control producing regard for others and a willing receptivity; and the other and more positive, that of self-development leading to increased personal power and achievement. It is still true that

"Self reverence, self knowledge, self control
These three alone lead life to sovereign power."

A full individual and social life is the crown of educational effort, for man's chief duty is ever "to assist his fellows and to develope his own higher self."

It is obvious that, at present, Elementary education cannot reach this high ideal. The pupils leave the Elementary school just as the social instincts are ripening. They are taught in huge classes. In the playground there is a scattered mob, in the class-room a multitude. It is difficult to establish or maintain individual relations even between pupil and teacher, almost impossible to secure them between individual pupil and Head Master.

The opportunities out of school hours when, with smaller numbers, more could be done, are not so numerous or so generally utilised as in schools of other types. There are not the school clubs, societies, guilds, and other social agencies of the Public school, the private High school or the public Secondary school. Economic reasons to a considerable extent prevent their formation. Organised games, nature study, visits to museums, have, it is true, done something in the Elementary school to make this loss less striking. Many individual teachers do all they can in this direction, and wish they could do much more : but here again, as previously in so many other ways we have shown, it is the large classes which hamper the most valuable features of school work and activity.

Further, one must admit with reluctance, it is true that such an extension of the duties of a teacher's vocation, as would impel him to make opportunities for work of this kind outside the formal limits of the school time table, is not generally welcomed. Many teachers feel that, having faithfully carried out all the lessons of the school curriculum, their work ought to be regarded as ended ; that their responsibilities are those of instruction, and ought not to be held as applying to more intimate relationships. They are willing to give *lessons* in anything you please, moral lessons, or lessons in citizenship included : but they fail to see why they

should be expected to give up their leisure for anything more personal or less formal than this. The
name *class teacher* is to some both a title and a
definition of duty.

Certain replies given to Miss E. P. Hughes
when she was preparing her report on the moral
education given in Wales four years ago are brutally
frank expressions of this view ;

1. "After school hours I prefer to have my
leisure to myself."

2. "I do not desire outside my teaching hours
to get into touch with my pupils."

3. "I don't believe in school functions out of
school hours."

4. "I never see the parents of my pupils."

5. "I should not care to see some of the
parents enter my school : it would do more harm
than good."

Such a feeling must be recognised and taken
into consideration in suggestions for reform. It
is a feeling that is more likely to grow under a
cast-iron officialdom and a driving of the teachers
by those in authority. Teachers do not believe
in compulsory volunteering. Many of them who
protest against such an arbitrary extension of their
duties, will yet be found to take up social work
where they are freer to act, and where they are
respected as independent helpers. It would be
unfortunate, however, if work of this kind, work
rich in promise for humanity and of a warmer

emotional tone, should be considered as against a code of professional honour. It is not beyond the resources of the profession to distinguish between altruism and advertisement.

There are, besides, many needs of the pupil of the Elementary school, that its kindest friends and most sympathetic servants think of great importance which lie a little outside the main scope of these suggestions. They imply really rather a co-operation of agencies for child-care than, in a strict sense, educational reform.

Sick, crippled, and poor children need greater attention. Medical treatment for the tuberculous, dental care, matters of feeding, cleansing, and clothing all cry out for a more generous consideration and our public conscience needs to be made more tender. "The Nation shall be saved by the breath of the school children," says the Talmud. "Saving the rates" is, with us, a more popular cry.

What can be done, then, to extend the influence of the Elementary school, especially having regard to the fact that so many pupils leave before 15 ?

This is really one of the great problems of the time. The raising of the school leaving age would do something. But there would still be the difficulty of guarding the years of adolescence. The suggestion of a compulsory continuation school course has been made. At present there are Voluntary Continuation Schools and Technical classes. But they are only partially successful in dealing with the problem. The Board of Education recognise that more must be done. "It is," they say, "in the failure of these classes to attract anything like a sufficient proportion of the possible students that the Board recognise *one of the weakest links in the educational system of the country.*"

Such classes are not only numerically weak, but they do not justify their title of "continuation," or fulfil the function so much to be desired of extending the influence of the school. By them is really established a new kind of evening school, which the pupil only attends for a short time. It has different teachers from those of the day school, not the same sense of corporate life, and is really but a *congeries* of classes. Sometimes it has a superintendent of classes, not often a Head in the same sense a day school has.

An attempt of recent years to make it more like a school, by insisting on definite courses of instruction, has gone some way in this direction, but has had many distinct disadvantages although regarded with the official favour of the Board of Education. It has kept students out who would have come for special instruction. It has driven pupils into certain classes against their will, and to the inconvenience of others who really wanted to work hard at certain subjects. It is, some consider, a device of formalism and of an official counsel of perfection. The same principle applied to another sphere would compel a man always to dine *table d'hôte* and never *à la carte*. As a principle of evening school instruction, it needs to be administered with considerable elasticity.

But it is certain that if the day-school hold could be more fully maintained, if the evening work could be associated with the former work of the school and the former teachers, the *continuation* would be more obvious.

There is no reason either why the element of healthy recreation should be banned. Day schools are usually bright nowadays, why should evening schools be so dull? The pupil who turns up at his old school to work in the gymnasium, or sing with a choral society, or to dance, or to read books and papers, or even, dare one say, to play at chess or billiards, is by each such attendance during his critical years more likely to become finally a good citizen. It would pay to increase the social clubs if you could thereby lessen the police. Perhaps the future Elementary school will have its *recreative annex* with a good gymnasium, a big room for dancing and meetings, a library, a reading room and a room for quiet games.

We have done much in this country by voluntary effort; boys' clubs of all kinds have been established although little has as yet been done for girls. Is it possible to do something more? In the Former Pupils' Guilds of co-education school girls have had equal privileges with boys to the mutual advantages of both. Could not there be a non-political, educational and recreative *ward-club* for both men and women in each district of our large cities? The school annexes would lead up to these.

In the field of Secondary education there is a better tradition, especially in the linking together of past and present pupils. It is, however, still true that the actual school life of pupils even of the most favourably circumstanced Secondary schools is lamentably short. The employers—the general public—are as we have seen largely to blame: and the parents have not sufficient faith in the real value of a good general education. Their readiness to believe that "the chance of a lifetime" in the matter of suitable employment may come when the boy is just turned 15 is pathetic. There are indications of a healthy reform in this direction, and the work of the Press, and of more intelligent leaders of industrial life is having a good effect. A sermon preached on the text of "a better chance for our youth" on every prize delivery platform might overcome the inertia of public opinion. Stamped agreements binding the parents to keep their children at school for a reasonably long course have been found effective in some areas. If one could bring to book the real offenders, the employers, for taking immature youth as for netting undersized fish, or killing game in a "close season," something might be done. And it would be amusing to find the Government itself, and Local Educational Authorities standing at the bar of public judgment "feeling their position" as the phrase runs "very keenly."

Within the Secondary schools themselves, the spirit of *esprit de corps* is increasingly developed. The Public schools issue rolls of their fellowships. The names of their soldiers, statesmen and scholars are on memorial brasses, their scholastic successes on scrolls "rich with the spoils of time." From time to time the leaders trained in the great schools go back again to distribute prizes on Speech Days and to ask with much appreciated thoughtfulness for a whole holiday. Scott and Oates have given a deeper glory to the public school, and by their gallantry have made every schoolboy in the land understand better and be prouder of the Public school tradition.

In the Municipal Secondary Schools the same kindling power of school patriotism is felt. The school honours board, when not used to give permanence to pettifogging successes, the school magazine, with its special Former Pupils page, and its record of all the work of the school in its wider sense, the same choral society, history society, sketching club or scout troop, etc., are all effective agencies in developing a spirit of fellowship. In many schools the school societies are a vital part of school activity and the honour of membership a real distinction.

The school past and present meets at Prize Givings. The athletic clubs of the school have their extension into Old Boys' Football and Cricket teams. The members of the Cadet Corps take up work with the Territorials. In many spheres of after-school life, in University, or bank, or shipping office, the youth who leaves school finds an older school-fellow who will help him in his new work. Letters from old pupils in distant parts of the world stir the imagination of the present school members, and hands are stretched out across the sea. Empire Day becomes a school reunion, and standing shoulder to shoulder an accomplished ideal.

With this appreciation of the Secondary school privileges the writer feels impelled to associate a warning. It will be a dangerous thing for the unity of the nation, if the favoured members of one class are given an extension of privileges, but are left ignorant of the duties and of the claims of social service. There is a real danger that Secondary *esprit de corps* enthusiasm and pride will serve to keep the ex-Elementary pupils separate in society from the ex-Secondary. And if, as we anticipate, all the best brains of the community are to get a Secondary school opportunity, this will tend to leave Elementary education "poor indeed." Robbed of its leaders, with lessened educational prestige, it will be impossible for its school pride, held to be so desirable, to be stimulated or maintained. Educational privilege, unless it is associated with public duty, will have a great centrifugal force driving the citizens of the commonwealth further apart in sentiment and social relationship. "Divide and rule" will not apply here. Education should unite.

This is Higher Education's most pressing social problem. An attempt to solve it has been made by the Public schools and Universities, in the way of University Settlements and special School Missions, which aim at linking in common interests extremes of the social scale. The Workers' Educational Association, of comparatively recent origin, is doing a great work in providing for the workers new opportunities of University education, which have been eagerly seized and fully utilised.

It will be harder still to link in mutual goodwill Elementary and Secondary pupils. The Board of Education fully realise the difficulty. In their report for 1911–12 they say :

"The problem, in common with numerous others arising from the wide extension of the scope of Secondary education in recent years, depends ultimately for its satisfactory solution on mutual understanding and co-operation between the teachers in Elementary and Secondary schools. It should be remembered that the historical development of education in England has rather tended to obscure the conception of its essential unity, and to create a feeling that the interests of Elementary and Secondary education are not merely distinct but even antagonistic."

Levelling up of Elementary school advantages will do something. A respect shown by Secondary schools for work done under less favourable circumstances than their own would do more. It ought to be possible to induce the pupils of the Secondary schools to take a kindly interest in their poorer brethren. Many ways of showing loving sympathy are open to them. A High school could take a school of special difficulty under its wing, provide concerts or entertainment for it, give the little ones a Christmas treat or a day in the country. Help in these directions if offered in the right spirit of brotherhood would be cheerfully accepted. Snobbery is the "lion in the path" of reform.

Then the Elementary and Secondary pupils may meet in the proposed ward clubs, or in the W. E. A. classes. An interesting club of a new type has recently been started in Liverpool under the aegis of the University. This club, open to both men and women over 18, for a subscription of 5s. a year gives admission to good reading and recreation rooms and library, and to lectures arranged by the University Extension Board in connection with the W. E. A. authorities. It has already proved the meeting place of the following sets of people :

(1)　University Graduates and Undergraduates.

(2)　Ex-pupils of a local Secondary school.

(3)　Ex-pupils of neighbouring Elementary schools.

Such a scheme is almost ideal in its possibilities of effective unity for the right objects. The club members have the benefits of recreation, fellowship and extended education.

If the various classes of the community are to be united, there must be a common basis of ideal. Here the work of the teaching of good literature in all grades of schools finds rich reward. If all pupils have learned to love the same books, they have already a bond of fellowship. It is still true that books

> ..."give
> New views to life, and teach us how to live;
> They soothe the grieved, the stubborn they chastise;
> Fools they admonish, and confirm the wise.
> Their aid they yield to all: they never shun
> The man of sorrow, nor the wretch undone;
> Unlike the hard, the selfish, and the proud,
> They fly not sullen from a suppliant crowd;
> Nor tell to various people various things,
> But show to subjects what they show to kings."

Books will not only give a common aesthetic enjoyment, but will give common ideals of life and conduct. They distil the spirit of humanity; so in loving the same books we love the same men and women who live in them or express themselves in them. In literature's "realms of gold," social distinctions are unknown.

But the greatest uniting force is, or ought to be, the religious teaching and moral training of the schools. If we unite on any ideal, it ought to be on that of personal conduct. It is, in the writer's judgment, cowardly to shirk a frank discussion of this most important subject. There is nothing, it is true, to be gained by stirring the waters of sectarian strife ; but there is everything to lose by confusing sectarian strife with religion. Christendom at least ought to unite in ideals of conduct founded on Christianity. The school ought to supply a twofold training :

(1) That of respect for one's own religion, and for one's own Church, its offices, its claims, its privileges.

(2) That of a respect for the religion, the Church and the consciences of others.

All Christian children may be united in reverencing the common ideals of Christendom—Jews and other non-Christian children being separately provided for. The class-room of the public school may become in this respect a model for the city. It should be so evident from the teacher's attitude towards religion, that he finds in it his own personal inspiration and that, as a member of a Christian Church, he himself takes a definite, if you like denominational, stand. Yet he must show, at the same time, that he is in love and charity with his neighbours, and teach the children the same lesson. With such an atmosphere in school, it would not be difficult to make provision outside its time-table for any definite denominational instruction, honestly demanded by the parents to supplement the ethical teaching of the school.

In practice there might be difficulties of detail

making such arrangements impossible. But the spirit of the school, and this is the main point, ought to show such a definite regard for religious influences and religious bodies that, in theory, supplementary denominational facilities would not be unwelcome.

The number of lessons on Christian ethics given each week in the school need not in the writer's opinion be many. A few lessons given with freshness and force are better than mechanical and routine performances. But they should show that the teacher himself, whatever be his religious denomination, is under the influence of a fully realised religion and holds it dear. If he cannot conscientiously do this he should not undertake the lessons.

And such teaching is for Christian folks best associated with the Bible. We are only now discovering the Bible as an instrument of religious education. It has been used as a book of history, and as a book of literature. Its least justifiable use is as a text book for examination purposes. It needs to be used as an inspiring guide to conduct.

Due selection of the Bible text for purposes of the instruction of youth ought to be made. The historical background of its older parts should be given. The Bible must be shown to be a book of life—dealing with real men and women. And with reverent and appreciative use it will never cease to charm and inspire. It would be a great national disaster if the Bible ceased to be used in schools, because some people place the importance of a dogmatic interpretation of its message above that of the message itself. Of all a teacher's privileges none is so high, so exacting, or so rich in reward as that which brings him into contact with the spiritual life of his pupils. The writer firmly believes with Mr Grant,

"It is not moral teaching that children really dislike, it is the appeal to insufficient motives. God is amazingly real and close to children, and they are constantly hearing His voice, and would continue to do so through life if we did not habitually sap their faith by appealing to worldly motives and letting it be only too apparent that we are influenced by worldly motives ourselves."

Fewer religious lessons, but these all given by teachers with a living faith in the Unseen, would be the highest reform of all.

We need to extend our ideal of efficiency. At present we have far too low and far too narrow views of what it should mean. The Greek ideal was one of efficiency, and yet it found room for loyalty, faith and reverence. At the end of his school education on entering upon civic manhood the Athenian youth, wearing the robe of citizenship, and being about to receive the soldier's shield and spear, made oath before the assembled citizens: "I will not dishonour my sacred arms ; I will not desert my fellow soldier, by whose side I shall be set; I will do battle for my religion and my country whether aided or unaided. I will leave my country not less, but greater and more powerful, than when she is committed to me ; I will reverently obey the citizens who shall act as judges ; I will obey the ordinances which have been established, and which in time to come shall be established, by the national will ; and whosoever would destroy or disobey these ordinances, I will not suffer him, but will do battle for them whether aided or unaided; and I will honour the temples where my fathers worshipped ; of these things the gods are my witnesses."

With this may be compared the suggested citizenship oath of the " Sons and Daughters of England," a society for social reconstruction aiming at joining in wise co-ordination, into a great Order, the workers for social reform.

" I promise to treat as brothers and sisters men and women of every religion and every country in the Empire; to make service the dominant ideal of my life, and therefore

"To seek the public good before personal advantage.

"To protect the helpless, defend the oppressed, teach the ignorant, raise the down-trodden.

"To be a good and loyal citizen of my municipality, the Motherland and the Empire.

"To all this I pledge myself in the presence of the Supreme Lord, and make promise to King,

Brotherhood and Country that I will be a true son (or daughter) of England."

Such inspiring pledges may, at least, be useful as an indication of those great ideals towards which the fuller revelation granted to us and our wider responsibilities should impel us. There may be many who would hesitate to ask for such solemn promises from the young ; but there are few who believe that our schools, our children, and ourselves would not be the better for following the ministry of service they indicate.

Perfection is unattainable, and reform is but a sign of life and growth. In this short sketch of the directions in which, to those engaged in teaching as a life's work, steps towards educational reform seem at present possible, many varying views are represented : but there is only one thing that will produce out of diversity of opinion a real educational unity. It is a sense of privilege in the doing of something, however little, to further "the safety, honour and welfare" of the children of the nation.

INDEX

www.ingramcontent.com/pod-product-compliance
Ingram Content Group UK Ltd.
Pitfield, Milton Keynes, MK11 3LW, UK
UKHW042142280225
455719UK00001B/36